CW00485920

Obsessed with KanYe West
Kanyeresa West

This book is dedicated to all the street performers who have an amazing talent. People will someday appreciate you for bringing fun in their boring ass day! This book is also dedicated to the person who would always say "do it girl" when I had some crazy idea, my cousin Danielle Buford.

Copyright (c)2013

All Rights Reserved

CONTENTS

Chapter One *Meeting Kanye West*

Chapter Two *Falling N Love With KanYe*

Chapter Three *My Sexual Fantasies of Kanye*

Chapter Four *Loving KanYe With All My Heart*

Chapter Five *The Making of Mrs. KanYe West*

Chapter Six *Giving My All To Kanye*

Chapter Seven *KanYe's Girlfriend's*

Chapter Eight *Watch The Throne*

Chapter Nine *The Media*

Chapter Ten *Kim Ye*

Chapter Eleven *Falling N Luv With Someone Else*

Chapter Twelve *Yeezy Taught Me*

CHAPTER ONE

"MEETING KANYE WEST"

Backstage, I saw him for the first time. There he was, Mr. KanYe West dressed in all white. For months I admired his pictures and bumped his music in my radio. I was so excited to meet him. When Kanye finally came in the room everyone began to clap. I do believe that I clapped first. We were at the Harold Washington Cultural Center. Kanye was there to judge my vocal performance, but first he performed his latest single "Gold Digger" while rocking the stage left to right, back and forth. Everyone backstage piled close together to see his performance. The crowd was going crazy inspired by the story behind Kanye. The day was July 31, 2005. He was about to release his second album, "Late Registration." So many people were inspired by him. In the beginning of his career he overcame the judgments of not being the typical hardcore gangsta rapper. He also didn 't wear the typical rapper clothing. Despite his short comings he turned out to be a very successful rapper. When kanYe merely died in a car accident years prior, he rapped a song about standing the test of time when his mouth was wired shut. The song called "Through The Wire" was Kanye's break-out song from his first album, "The College Dropout". Meeting Kanye West was a great experience. I remember thinking "wow that's Kanye West"! "What an amazing guy"! Although Kanye had his claim of fame from producing hits for artists like Alicia Keys, Jay-Z and Jermaine Dupri, just to name a few, he had just recently became his own solo act.

Kanye started out as a rapper in Chicago and began to make hip hop beats in the late 90's. He moved to New Jersey and New York to accomplish his goals to become a successful rapper and producer. He became a producer for Rocafella Records but wanted to rap more than anything. Kanye isn't the type of guy who deserves to be in the background. He's the guy that needs to be on the center stage. He wanted to do what he loved and that beyond making beats was rapping. Kanye overlooked doughts and stereotypes and became one of the biggest hip hop rappers of our time.

When he first made it as a solo artist, I remember thinking how cool that was. I didn't know much

about Kanye at first because when his first solo album was released, I was only listening to Gospel music. Because of that I didn't know much about what was going on in the hip hop world. When I first heard Jesus Walks, I was so head over heels in love with the lyrics and the beat. Ya see, the beat itself gives so much amazing energy. I can remember wondering while I was doing gospel music "would I be able to be successful that genre"? Well, there's a line in the song Jesus Walks that says, *"but if I talk about God my record won't get played huh? But I hope it take away from my sins and be the day I'm dreaming bout". Those lyrics gave me motivation to do me, no matter what that was, gospel or r&b.* Every song that Kanye was releasing was from his soul and it made people like me love him. He wasn't creating money marketing songs, but songs from the heart. He was making songs that people could relate to.

I still speak from my soul, Diamonds, KanYe West

Kanye West was loved by everyone. The white audience, the black audience and so many people respected him because he added something that hip-hop was missing. Even thou his CEO Jay-Z was also lyrical, a lot of people related to Jay at the time from his street cred topics. Kanye had a different flow. Kanye spoke about how its best to follow your heart vs. what's popular. He would encourage people to do what the fuck they wanted to do. Jay was the kind of rapper to speak similar but from a different lifestyle. Kanye was known as the overlooked kid, while Jay was known for coming from a project-hood lifestyle.

They both are great artists. Jay-Z was known since the 90's and Kanye was just coming out. When I met Kanye he was just releasing his second album so he was new and fresh to the world. He was a new artist with a new flow. He won the heart of America and then some. When Kanye was was done performing "Gold Digger" he took a seat in the front row.

Soon it was time for me to perform. I was nervous, shaking and did not want my nerves to show. I was a tough performer then. At that time being a tough female was in. Popular female artists like Missy Elliot, Brooke Valentine and Fantasia all shared their own unique tough girl images. Music, image and style have an effect on everyone who listens and watches. We become inspired and it becomes the "it" thing, which is the thing we call a "fad". As much as we can say that we created our own image, it somehow branded from an icon of some sort.

I was wearing things like hats and a lot of bracelets, but I kept it sexy, wearing fitted jeans. At that time I didn't put too much into my apparel, but performing in front of Kanye was different. The fashion school on State Street in Chicago provided me with a $400 voucher to shop at Nordstrom for this event. But yo, I prefer shopping at rainbow with $100. At Rainbow there are colorful fitted clothing to choose from and at Nordstrom their clothing is basic brown, blue and black attire.

However, I still managed to buy something sexy. I picked out a brown silk shirt, some tight fitted jeans and some brown slacks. I guess it'll do, I thought. I mean, what could I say? It was free money and free clothes, so I didn't complain and played grateful. Knowing that I was performing in front of Kanye West gave me more of a reason to try something new.

I'm the best dressed next to fags, KanYe West

When it was time for me to sing I was so excited to be standing in front of him. The song that I decided to sing was "So High" by John Legend. While performing I would only glance at kanYe, but I could see him from the corner of my eye. I didn't want to show him how much I liked him and I was trying hard not to blush. I kept my eyes glued into the crowd. At the end of the song I sang an accapella verse from KanYe's song "We Don't Care", adding my own twist to it.

"Singing on the subway just to get by, stack yo money to we get sky high, I wasn't pose to make it out D.C.F.S jokes on them I'm at my best, and we don't care what people say."

When I was through performing, people applauded. I looked at Kanye as he spoke good things about me. Over the mic he was telling me how great I was. I was so hyped even thou I didn't show it. I was concerned about what he may say, and he said nothing but great things. Because it was coming from him, it made me feel real good!

He told me "I had star power, star presence and worked the stage like a pro". I felt so special. My ego got bigger after hearing that. It was coming from Kanye West and that felt great. If I didn't believe in my dreams before, now I really believed in them. Before he left the building, he touched my shoulder, starring into my eyes. Can we say love at first sight? I had love anxiety. Feeling a rush every day, wanting to see him again. I thought to myself, there has got to be a way. So from that day fourth I was determined to make it into Kanye West arms. I had so many reasons why. Beyond the fact that he was talented, smart and edgy, he was also sexy and gully. He turned me the fuck on! A humble, yet cocky dude. Confidence is great, but not too much where you forget people. But because he was humble that drove me to want him. I was intrigued I must admit because of his seat in the hip hop world, I won't frunt. I wanted to be with him and where he was. It was my dream since forever! But I was also heavily attracted to him. I don't like working with people who I don't feel I could vibe with. I liked Kanye. Knowing how much I liked him drove me to want him to be the one who would make my dreams come true.

Kanye and I thought a lot alike. I took my teddy bear with me places when I was 18. For Kanye's logo to be a teddy bear when he was 28, I felt right at home liking him. I was feelin the way he visualized art. Anyone could tell that Kanye was an out the box thinker. It was cool being his fan because I think outside the norm too.

I don't want to grow up, I'm a grown ass kid –KanYe West, Through The Wire

Around the time that we met he released his single "Gold Digger". The lyrics related to people and the beat was sampled from Ray Charles. The song was very catchy. So many people in this world experienced people being with them for only money and for Kanye to make a song on that subject was 100% awesome. It had a funny yet true message to it. August 29, 2005 was the release date of Kanye West sophomore Album, "Late Registration". It was different from his first album. His first album, "The College Dropout" had a soulful hip-hop sound. It was full of soulful beats sampled from old school music. The sophomore album was different thou. It had a sound rich mixed with strings and violins. When his first album came out people appreciated his music because he related to everyone. He spoke about regular life. But by the second album his lyrics were different. Because his life was different I'm sure people would expect his words to shift. The second album was about being a rap star and staying a rap star. Either way being a Kanye West fan wasn't boring because it was like following the story of his life.

What made the new album even more awesome is when he toured the U.S, October 10, 2005. He had background singers and an orchestra with a rich sound of violins and horns. Like me, I can tell that Kanye dared to be different. I loved that about him! You never knew what great idea he was going to come up with next. I'm sure all Kanye fans were on the edge of their chair never knowing what Kanye would do next. Although we believed that it would be something great. In time it became a wonder to the world of what funny or out of the ordinary thing Kanye would say or do next. He began to speak his mind in places most people would keep quiet. For example, he went on a live telecast sharing his feelings on President Bush. Eventually, people were learning that Kanye was the kind of person to speak his mind. From his outbursts at award shows and live broadcasts, Kanye would say what he felt. No matter where Kanye was, they would catch him off camera and on camera keepin it real. In Kanye's lyrics he's also blunt. People related and appreciate him for his voice in the hip-hop community.

Kanye was gaining a big name, being a different hip-hop artist. He was a rising star. There are many hip-hop artists that have tried to make a million or have tried to keep a famous name and failed after one hit. But every year Kanye was gaining more, more and more. He was making more hits, getting more fame and making more money.

He had a big tour outside the country with the popular rock band "U2", early 2006. Even thou Kanye traveled Paris, London, and other countries prior, this was his big tour outside the U.S.

Because Kanye is very talented and unique, that put him in a place that most rappers never got the chance to go to. At the time he was dating Brooke Crittedom, a model who began working for MTV after hooking up with him. After he toured with U2 it was rumors that they were broken up. I was always so sure that they'd stay together because Kanye seemed to be the type that would keep the same girl like his best friend, Jay-Z. They came to an end anyway. Around the same time that Kanye broke up with Brooke, he had a concert in New York, at Bryant Park. I was excited about both. I was happy he was done with his girl and I was excited that he was in concert in the U.S again.

For the first time I traveled to New York. At the concert Kanye wore a blue and white shirt, looking good. He began throwing towels in the audience while performing "Number One" with Pharell. I felt the only people important there were me and him. As always people cheered and were so in love with Kanye's performance. I was in no way intimidated.

When I left the concert, I headed straight to Chicago for his next concert held at the Congress Theatre. The concerts were days apart from each other and I just had to be at each one. I purchased an orange outfit with some orange shoes to go with it. I have to look fly and do better than these other hoes. No one's going to outdo me. Shit they couldn't even try.

Kanye was set to perform at 7:00 p.m. but what time did Kanye start performing? 10:00 p.m! But because he's Kanye West people waited around and was still full of energy when he finally came out on stage. He started the show performing "Get Em High" with Common.

"My flow is in the pockets I can't call it, I got the swerve like alcoholics" Kanye West, Get Em High

I wanted to be closer to Kanye. I wanted to be backstage with him again. I was enjoying myself nonetheless. Everyone was so hyped to see him perform. He was wearing some dark shades and a colorful shirt, looking sexy as fuck. I saw the women that wanted him and was thinking, "they don't stand a chance"! See I know me. If anything I'm good at, I'm good at standing out. I knew that I could be the one that Kanye noticed, and not them. My confidence was always sky high. I believed in me as someone that I am and also someone that I wasn't, but could be. There was also an extra boost in my confidence from the responses I received on a daily basis singing on the subway.

Since April 2004, I would sing for money on the subway in Chicago, on Jackson Street. I would pick my favorite popular song and sing it with all the passion in the world. People began to realize that even thou I wasn't singing my own songs, I was singing from the heart. People's comments reassured me that. I became accustomed to love and affection from people while performing. I felt I deserved it anyway because I'm super talented. I believed because I was popular in the city Kanye was from, it only felt right for us to be a union some kind of way, one day.

I, like most American woman want to be number one. We don't want to be at Diane Ross status, the famous singer in love with a married man. We want to be Beyoncé's. We want to be treated like a queen in every way. So even thou I wanted Kanye to sign me, I also wanted him to be my man. I wanted him to see me as a queen and nothing less. That night I didn't get to be with Kanye as I hoped. I didn't make much effort either, but it was still a wish. I was so in love with him so I eventually wanted it to happen. So many things happened after meeting Kanye West. I met very interesting people. Just a week later I attended a barbecue with John Legend. Now, I had a crush on John Legend right before I met Kanye, but by the time I met John those feelings were gone. I'm one of those all or nothing chic's. I'm too loyal for my own good. Even thou I wasn't Kanye West girl or profiting from none of those feelings, I wasn't about to flirt with his friend. I also took a chance turning down my career for my feelings. One of the guys on John Legend's team offered me to go on tour with him, but I refused. It's because I didn't want to come off as a whore. I also didn't think that Kanye West would be support something like that. I felt I was worthy enough of a more direct approach. I was not use to secrecy or trying to figure things out. I was more of a direct chic, so you would have to come off as such. Once I met Kanye, I wanted him to know how much of a good girl I was. So if word came out that I was at this private barbecue with John, I wanted Kanye to know that I turned something like that down and wasn't a groupie chic.

And here it was another day. I was singing on State Street in Chicago when I met radio personality, Dj Kool-Out. Kool-Out pulled over in his car and handed his card to me. He told me that he wanted me to record an intro for his show on Wgci. Of course I was up for it. I recorded the track and made it happen. There I was once again over the air ways of Wgci. This time it was my music that people heard, not just my voice. What an exciting experience. I can't count how many times I appeared on Wgci, my favorite radio station. I'll get to that in a minute. First let me talk about a similar experience I had.

I remember meeting No. I.d. No I.d is a well known producer in Chicago. At the time I didn't know that this was the guy who taught Kanye how to make beats when Kanye was younger. All I knew is he was this popular producer. He wasn't Kanye so I wasn't trying to hear what he was talking about. He walked away with this "I could have helped you attitude" like most boogie people do when I turn them down. It's okay, cause I didn't feel I needed him so, so what. I think a lot about those moments now thou. I wonder was Kanye behind those approaches and I never knew because I was too dam stubborn to let my guard down.

My dad who loves me dearly wasn't too fond of my crush on Kanye. He as most men see a career path a lot healthier with one focusing on self, not surrounding your hopes into someone else. I know my dad meant well wanting me to not be all about Kanye, but if he could feel how I was feeling, maybe he would have eased up on me about things. He was quick to email me the news that Kanye had proposed to Alexis Phifer. At the time I was so hurt because of where the news came from. It came from my favorite person, my dad. The guy who was mostly impressed by me and my goals. On top of that, the news itself was surprising. I walked about three miles or more listening to music trying to grasp the information. I wanted Kanye to love me, nothing less. Proposal meant marriage and marriage meant that I couldn't be first. I was 24 years old and yea I've had celebrity crushes before, but this was different. I believed in the chance to be with Kanye West. However, I think my odd behavior was encouraged by how I met my dad. I grew up believing that the impossible could be possible. I met him all from a wish and got closer to him by doing a lot of waiting. I got him to be the dad in my life from a simple wish. The man I call dad was not my dad from birth and not from adoption.

At the age 10, I ran away from a group home that was located in Desplaines, IL. I was a ward of the state since birth due to neglect. I lived in group home after group home and foster home after foster home. When I ran away, I didn't plan on going to a radio station, but I was bored while riding the Red-Line, C.TA. I asked random people on the train where Wgci was located. People were nice, told me directions, but were very curious. While they were curious, I was full of hope and couldn't wait to get there. At the time Wgci was not only the most popular urban radio station, but it also had the number one ratings throughout the entire city. Majority African Americans who liked rhythm and blues probably preferred Wgci over the rest of the choices. Other radio stations provided old school, pop and rock music. And pop wasn't the same as today. I remember turning to a radio station in Chicago called B96 in the 90's. It was one song every thirty minutes that was enjoyable for me. I wasn't one of the percentage listening to old school music at that age. I preferred listening to new music like the mass majority that was making Wgci number one. In other words Wgci was what was poppin!

When I arrived there was a door locked and you couldn't get passed it without the Secretary letting you in. A lady, I assumed who was the Secretary came to the door. I was bluntly honest when I told her that I wanted to sing. She asked me my age and the whereabouts of my parents. I was honest about that also. Eventually, she let me inside. After leaving me for a few minutes, she came back in and allowed me to sing to the people in the office. Everyone was so nice. They applauded and asked questions about my love for music and who my favorite artist was. I told them that I was into Monica. They smiled. I was not only at the most popular radio station in Chicago, but I was singing to very important people. I was so excited for all the possibilities that could come. I felt so special with how they were treating me. It was a care so new.

They introduced me to some of the popular radio personalities like Doug Banks, Jean Sparrow and Crazy Howard McGhee. I was smiling not knowing that it was so easy to get this special treatment from the people at Wgci. People would go crazy just to be on the phone with them and there I was amongst their presence. Those same people were signing t-shirts for me. They were even giving me cd's. The former president of Wgci, Marv Dyson gave me my first set of headphones after giving me a great intriguing speech of how special those kind of headphones were. It was the kind that only gave you

F.M radio. In my mind, I was thinking, “I won’t ever turn it from Wgci”. I couldn’t understand the love. It was so overwhelming, but I embraced it. I was thinking to myself, no one ever treats me this good, so please don’t stop. Then I was given this long lecture about my safety from the Secretary whose name was Princess Pearl. She and Promotional Manager, Carmen brought me lunch and showed a heavy concern for me. They gave me their number to keep in touch before returning me home. I, to this day can never forget one of the most special days of my life.

That was the end of that. But it wasn’t the end of the story. As I listened to my headphones every day I was getting use to the radio personalities on Wgci. Rick Party, the disk jockey who was on air from 6-10 weeknights on Wgci was my favorite. He was funny and very loving with his audience. I started to anticipate hearing his show every night. I asked Carmen from Wgci if I could meet him. She told me that I would have to call him during his show and have permission from my group home to do so.

December 1, 2005 I called the radio station during his show. It rang, it rang and it rang. Finally when he answered I asked, “Rick Party can I meet you”? He with no hesitation said, “sure you can, can you hold on for a second”? I replied “yes”. As he put me on hold, I jumped up and down, so excited. Finally after so many minutes later he put me back through the line and told me that I could come to the radio station during his next show. I was so full of joy. I felt so lucky. I didn’t expect these things to be so easy. Everything before then seemed hard.

At this time I had nobody. I didn’t have any stable friends. I was a ward of the state living in D.C.F.S custody and was moving left to right. I never got the chance to get close to anyone. I didn’t have any family so being able to go to the radio station meant so much more than just music.” Maybe he could be my mentor”, I thought. After going through very small changes to get permission, I was able to go. I was so excited. Boy, did I know all the things that were coming next.

That following Monday, December 4, 1995 at 6p.m I met the number one Radio Personality in Chicago, Rick Party. A staff named Riquia who worked in the group home that I lived in accompanied me. We were waiting in the lunch area, when Rick Party's co-host First Lady came in to buy a soda and noticed that we were there. We let her know that we were waiting to meet Rick. She gladly walked us in. Wow he was cute! I wasn't use to seeing guys that were clean cut and dressed nice like that. I remember thinking "he sound chocolate". He should've been doing TV. He shouldn't be hiding his face in radio. I was so gully and he was so caring. He asked me questions about myself and I let him know how much I loved music. I impressed him when I showed him a folder of the songs that I wrote.

During the stay of my visit, I had so much fun. But when he even let me sing on the radio that was my favorite moment! I saw him be the best radio personality that ever walked. He was funny and quick with his hands on the switchboard. He would change his voice and tease people, but would also show so much love and passion with them. He was such a pro when it came to his job. First Lady, his co-host was a good partner with him. Those two together made a great show.

As our night ended he gave me the number to the special line that I could call when he was at the radio station. Riquia, the staff took the number instead. I played it cool, but was thinking, "he gave that to me, not you"! That day was amazing. I bragged about my day afterwards and was so happy. My dream was to be a singer by the time I was Monica's age. At the time she was 14 and I was only 12. I felt that it was possible, especially by the way things were going. But what I didn't know was that I was about to get a family and not a record deal. And if I could turn back the hands of time, I wouldn't change a thing.

Eventually, Rick Party grew to know me. I also grew to know his sister and his mom. I would call him dad and he would treat me like his daughter. In time, I moved in with his mom. When he moved to Georgia I was sad, but he flew me there to be with him and his other children Christmas, 1997. I met all 6 of his children and they embraced me with no problem. They didn't mind me being their big sister and I was very happy that I didn't have to prove myself to any of them.

In 1998, me and my grandmother flew to Georgia to meet our additional family, Evander Holyfield and his family. He had recently married one of my aunts. So you know how I was feeling, right? I went from not having a family at all to having a great and well-known family. I went from feeling hopeless to feeling complete. Through every experience I had with my new family, I wouldn't trade it in for money. Yea, I wanted to be a great singer and was inspired to be, but it is what it is and it was what it was. Even before my dad moved to Georgia I refused to go out on the fun activities with the group home that I lived in. I preferred to listen and tape my dad's entire show. Rick was all I had before I met his family. To know that I knew him and to know that he loved me, sticking by my radio made me feel like I belonged to something and someone. I had so much fun listening to his show and I even added fun to it. Not only would I tape his show, I started writing down in alphabetical order the artists name and the songs played daily. I also kept up with the Coke 9 at 9. The Coke 9 at 9 was a part of the show that started at 9p.m. During that part of the show they would play 9 of the most requested songs. I loved it!

When he moved to Georgia it was very lonely for me. I began to write him every day the things that I would do and experience. Writing him letters made me feel better while he was gone. I felt loved. I felt like we were still in touch. We continued to talk every day and that made me feel better too. I couldn't frunt thou, I always felt special. He would play interviews that he had with famous stars and I could tell he enjoyed being on the phone with me.

I remember walking and talking like I was the shit in my group home and at school. I not only had someone who cared for me, but someone at his magnitude care for me. I went from wondering who cares to "oh I'm so happy someone cares". I was big headed at times about it. I think I got big headed when I would wonder. Those were probably the days that I missed him the most. Cockiness is always a frunt in my opinion. It's the moment your standing alone and try to appear great. Being great is just that, being great. But I did come off cocky at times.

After getting close to my dad, I grew a crush on Teddy Riley. I wanted to meet him and I didn't really know why. All I know is I was in love with his facial features and his music. But I know that after wanting to meet him, I eventually did. It was a very chill moment. He even signed a paper for me. I didn't jump all over him like I thought I would, but I can't lie I was super happy.

With these experiences going through the back of my head as an adult, I can remember when all I did was believe. I remember some of my wishes coming true. So, when it comes to Kanye West that's where I was with impossible walls. I didn't see the walls. I saw the wall down. I didn't know exactly how to take the walls down, I just knew that they were possible to come down. I knew that it was possible to see Kanye West again. I knew that it was possible to be his girl.

However, now that Kanye was engaged I wasn't sure how to feel. My first mind said fuck it all, but somehow in time I began to love him enough to trust him for a record deal. I went from wanting to be his queen to accepting that I may end up being his Diane Ross. When I say "be his Diane Ross" I'm speaking of how Diane Ross as a lot of woman in the industry were head over heels in love with their producer or CEO of some sort, and yet were the side chic because he was married. So these women would love the shit out of their boss yet had to accept that they weren't number one. I didn't want to be second best as I'm sure those women didn't either. But, I loved Kanye too much to let go.

It was late 2007, and there was silence from Kanye. We hadn't heard new music. Fans like me wanted to hear more. He was mostly just appearing at events with his fiancé, Alexis. Now at the time I was living with my God-mom. She was helping me and thought that I was in school. Little did she know I was going to school only to keep up with Kanye news on a daily basis. I guess when I see something that is all I see. I saw myself getting a record deal somehow and nothing less. I had a vision and I only saw that. I didn't see the need to get an apartment. I didn't see the need in getting caught up with regular life. I felt my focus should stay on my career. I didn't want to look back and see that I dreamed but did not invest in that dream. I didn't put any effort in other men, housing or simple shit people worry about. I didn't mind sacrificing by giving my all to my career. I was 24, not dating, and not having any fun. I was just focused on my career and Kanye. I wanted him to be the one to make it all happen. I stopped auditioning and just looked to him. Most people would feel that a woman should have a condo and a college degree by that time but in my mind it would all get better soon. I didn't see things staying the way that they were. I also didn't mind skipping school for the hopes of something much bigger. I really felt like I needed to keep my eye on Kanye Omari West.

CHAPTER TWO

"FALLING IN LOVE WITH KANYE WEST"

What I would not to do to be with this guy? What I would not do to see him again? I was so caught up into Kanye West that when his videos came on TV, it was like he was talking to me.

I'm on TV talking like it's just you and me Can't Tell Me Nothing, Kanye West

Whenever I saw his face anywhere rather it was a magazine, interview, or on one of his videos, I would light up because I was so into him. Anything Kanye West said in my opinion made sense. I was in love with his music, his style and everything. Something in the back of my thoughts would say he reminds me of an ex, but I ignored it because Kanye was my hero. I saw everything that I wanted to see, and that was a man of value. Kanye didn't have a bunch of tattoos or piercings. In my opinion he was a simple guy who happened to be a lyricist. I liked Kanye for his looks, his style, his music, his videos and because he was so outspoken. Kanye reminded me so much of me. He was edgy, hyper and artistic. I just loved him. I was so excited Spring 2007 when there was new music released by Kanye. It was a snippet of the first single for his third album. I played that 30 second snippet over and over. The song was called "Can't Tell Me Nothing". Omg! It was so soulful!

I was on the computer doing my usual, keeping up with Kanye's news and it was posted everywhere that Kanye was releasing a new single for his upcoming album. The song was only 30 seconds and I was eager to hear the rest.

I was still alone and single watching Kanye date Alexis Phifer picture after picture, news after news. I was still in hopes to see Kanye someday. If I was just some regular girl, I don't know how I would feel. I always kept the day that Kanye and I met in the back of my mind. I felt even if it was just for music, I believed in the chance to be around him in real life someday. I just had to figure out how, when and where. I wasn't really planning. I would just wondering how we would see each other again. I'm classy. Even thou I had my ways of getting what I wanted, going out and getting it, I wasn't so desperate to behave like a groupie. I was too cocky to do all that. I never planned to wait for him outside his tour bus or concerts. If I was going to do something, it would be absurd yet great. It would be something never forgotten. His new album was due in July. But I wasn't surprised when it wasn't released until September.

I'll be late for that. I'll be there in 5 minutes. 5 minutes later, I'll be there in 5 minutes

Late, KanYe West

Being late became the intro of whatever Kanye would do. Why? I'm not sure but I learned to be patient when it comes to Kanye West. But in the end I was never disappointed. September 11, 2007, KanYe's third album "Graduation" was released. I was so happy! The cd cover was animated and made the excitement of first listening to it fun. The music was so amazing. Somehow 50 cent released his album the same day. I still to this day never heard it. If he was beefing with Kanye, he was beefing with me. I loved Kanye beyond anyone could know. I would take up for him at the drop of a hat. As usual I loved Kanye's album. I was talking about the album and was feeling the album a whole lot. My favorite song was "Flashing Lights". Flashing Lights was a very soft side of Kanye. That was the side that I was in love with, the guy who told his heart. Now "The Glory" was another song on the album. On that song he talked about how he wanted to continue to be a rising star. He also talked about making money and keeping the best of the best. As much as that sounds good and I was feeling the song, I was more into the guy who wanted more than he had. See the gully side of Kanye comes from a humble place, but the side that Kanye has it all comes from an arrogant place. I loved the humble yeezy. We all have both sides. It's up to us to choose which side were going to let lie dormant.

Three months later, after writing a beautiful book and being one of the greatest moms ever, especially to the hip hop community, Donda West, Kanye West's mom passed away. This was sad for the world to hear. Not only was this one of the hip-hop moms, but this was a woman who was in the fore-front speaking greatness. Kanye showed off his mom and showered her many times and many places with star treatment. People grew to know her. During that time it was sad to hear and sadder to watch Kanye endure this. But just like when he rapped with his mouth wired shit, he bounced back and continued his tour. The decision to continue his tour made a lot of his fans respect him even more. Hey, we would have understood if he canceled it, but because he continued it we loved him for it. It said a lot about how much his fans meant to him. It was therapy for him too, giving him the platform to express how he was feeling.

To put more icing on the cake, sarcastically speaking, it hadn't even been 2 years that Kanye was engaged to Alexis, but yet just that quick, they split. I really denied the news when I first read it. I was thinking, yea right! Did I want that? Yes, I really did. I just didn't believe it after the media and Kanye put up such a big image of their relationship. I'm thinking, "okay maybe the first girl and Kanye didn't make it, but not this one". Kanye seemed to me an amazing guy who was very passionate with women. I felt that if he made you number one he would crown you his queen and never let you go. I also felt that he would never let you go if he held you close. I finally realized that the break-up news was right. After all the pictures and trips that he took with this woman, I was just so very surprised that it was true.

It was 2008 and I traveled to Miami to catch some sun. It was my first trip to Miami and I'm glad I took the trip. It was hot there when it was cold in Chicago. I called back home just to brag about the weather. But you know I was so in love with Kanye that I didn't want other men. I was in the hot sun at the Martin Luther Day Parade having so much fun. I was careful thou because I didn't want to get close to other guys. So I didn't get too comfortable. I was hoping that when I saw Kanye again he'd see how tight my pussy was. I wanted him to feel my loyalty while making love. I felt that if I got close to another guy I would forget Kanye and my dreams. I was trying my best not to get too wrapped up into things or people. I didn't want to get pregnant again. I didn't want to forget about my dreams and get too involved in something else, so I kept my eyes and heart on Kanye West.

It was April, 2008 when I traveled to Seattle to see Kanye during his tour. I think without me wanting to admit it, I was becoming a groupie. Here it was Year 3 and he had yet to invite me out. I began to do what it took slowly to get to Kanye. He knew who I was that's for sure. We spoke a couple of times after meeting, but wasn't much said. I always had some kind of reason why him not being in my life was delayed. Hope is the reason why I held on.

Ironically the tour ended on my birthday, June 13. I won't share why I think so, but I will say that what me and Kanye had was phenomenon for years. As much as I wanted someone to kiss me, hold me and touch me, the little things we were doing to inspire each other kept me to wait for him.

I didn't want to have sex with other guys and I surely didn't want a boyfriend. I only wanted Kanye to touch me eventually. I would keep up with him and believe that he would come on a horse one day and rescue me. I really was hoping he would say how much he loved me the entire time that I waited for him. Some people would think it's absurd to wait for Kanye West, especially that's its Kanye West the famous superstar. I guess when you wait for your mother for 11 years with a window of hope, not knowing for sure the outcome, it can be kind of normal for you to wait for people. Everyone becomes accustomed to childhood habits. Just like the military break men out of their normal behavior, so can people break habits on their own. It's just that as an adult, unlike childhood it's your choice to do what you want. So since you don't have someone giving you orders, a lot of times people become set in their ways because it's easier to just be themselves. Point is, when you're an adult you want to do what you want to do and as much as I could've made attempts to meet handsome men, I wanted Kanye.

I'm stubborn like that. I see things just like I see it and no other way. I waited for my mom 11 years. There were people who told me that my mom could come back and get me anytime if she wanted to. To know that I believed what I wanted to believe, especially with the window of opportunity still open. To me it was more than possible for my mom to come back and get me, I just never knew when. I waited and waited and waited until the day I realized my mommy didn't love me enough to come back for me. I didn't even believe it until they told me that she couldn't come back. I was 11 years old by that time. For the first 11 years of my life I only hoped for love, but wasn't truly loved. So I am who I am because of that. That situation molded me. That's the way I loved for 11 years.

I repeated that same behavior shortly after. After I met my dad and he moved to Georgia, I didn't want to have a boyfriend like I once did. I loved my dad so much that I wanted to belong to him. I was more sure about waiting for him because I knew that my dad did care. I wanted to live with him and have a family of my own. I wanted to belong.

I was accustomed to waiting for something that I wanted, instead of moving on to someone new. It made it easier to love, hoping that Kanye would come back to Chicago.

When I met Kanye West and fell in love with him despite how hard it seemed to get to him, I didn't give up. All I knew is that all I wanted was him. So I waited, planned, cried, hoped, wished and stayed loyal, doing whatever it took to get KanYe West in my life. I was so sexually satisfied. I would play with my pussy every night and imagine Kanye inside of me. I would take all of his music and put it towards me and him. I was in love with him. I couldn't see past me being with him. I didn't even want to phanthom the thought of us not being together. It's all I wanted. It's all I needed. Despite every year that went by when I should have lost hope, I held on to my faith.

I didn't speak much about it to anyone. My mom and dad was the only ones that knew I loved Kanye. The woman that I call mother is the mom that adopted me after meeting Rick Party. I embraced her since my dad couldn't keep a girlfriend. I attached to her after meeting her at church. My mom knew that I was head over heels in love with Kanye. She also knew how bad I wanted him. She knew how dedicated I made my life to him. She felt that it didn't make much sense, but she also knew why I made those decisions. Like I said, her and my dad were the only ones who knew this information. Others knew I liked him, but for the most part no one really knew just how bad I was in love with him. But one day my mom told me "one day, Kanye is going to drive you crazy". At the time I disagreed. However, the fact is, is that it would have been better if I fell in love with someone close, someone I could fuck every night. Kanye knew how much I loved him and he could have reached out to me. He could have even snapped me out of my faith in him and told me he planned on dating someone else each time. Because of how I loved during my childhood, I repeated that same fucking behavior. Waiting for someone, hoping for someone and all I really wanted each time was to not wait, and not hope. I wanted to be loved right then and there. I would wait and I would hope. Each time I did not know how long I was going to be waiting. If I could turn back the hands of time, I would have preferred being in love, not chasing love.

CHAPTER THREE

"MY SEXUAL FANTASIES OF KANYE WEST"

I waited for Kanye. I longed for kanYe. I was always eager to see him. I never knew when that would be, but I was always in high hopes. I always told myself the reason that I didn't spend time with him was because of of how busy he was. I told myself for years and years that. I felt it would be only a matter of time before he was bending me over and fucking me. We were growing as we were getting to know each other. I believed I was better than the girls he was dating since we hadn't become intimate yet. Besides, he proved me wrong when I thought he and Brooke would be together for such a long time and yet the relationship ended. The way he courted and treated her, how they were always spending time together seemed so everlasting. It shocked me to see Kanye leave Brooke and propose to another woman just months later. I assumed Kanye was talking to this chick also while he was dating Brooke. So, I never knew where our conversations would lead. I wasn't patient with Kanye. I was always upset with him that he wasn't where I wanted him to be.

Then I thought about it, "how patient can a girl be"? A girl's got needs. But yet, I had this overwhelming lust for him and stayed true.

Prior to falling for Kanye, two years straight I had sex with my best friend Kevin almost every day. After falling for Kanye I stopped fucking him. I want to say we stopped making love because that's what we were doing. I was in love with Kevin right before I looked to Kanye to heal my broken heart. I had no idea when I was loving Kanye that it would be so long before I could see him again. I became accustomed to keeping my pussy for him. It became a lifestyle to sing on Jackson Street and go home. I didn't want to have fun with people that I knew. I didn't want to visit the hot spots in town because I was so focused on "when was Kanye coming to see me". His silence was really the reason for it all. I just never knew.

Where are you Yeezy? Kanye West, Flashing Lights

I didn't lose my virginity until I was 18 years old, so I masturbated my entire childhood. When my dad came into my life, I did what I could to please him as a daughter. I ran away from one of my foster homes to see this boy and my dad threatened to fly into town and hurt him if he touched me. I felt so special and I didn't want to let him down. I began living my life as a Christian for most of my teenage years. As much as I loved and admired my dad I was more into girls as a kid then boys. I'm sure it was because I was around girls more than boys. Most foster homes and group homes isolated me from having any fun except if I was with my family or a group gathering. So I fantasized a lot.

I didn't get to see much porn as a kid. I would create fantasies with my imagination. Sometimes in order for me to have an orgasm I would think real nasty thoughts. After falling for Kanye, the more I didn't have sex, the more I wanted Kanye. The more I didn't go out and have fun, the easier it was for me to wait for Kanye. I didn't pursue a life of my own, I just preffered pursuing a life with Kanye. I actually enjoyed it because I envisioned Kanye and I together one day. I just never knew when. I'd go home when my day was done, get under my covers and come all over myself thinking of Kanye West.

It all started with his sexy ass "Gold Digger" video. That video was played so much on MTV. It came on one day when I was alone at my friend's house. I jumped up and down on the couch in excitement. He looked so good to me in that video. His swagger was a plus. I was in love with his confidence. As I watched it I got under the covers and imagined that all those girls were me. I imagined me touching him, kissing and caressing him. I imagined him biting my neck and telling me how bad he wanted me. I came so fast and so good. I'd take my finger, wet it and lick it, then rub it slowly around my pearl. Thoughts running through my mind, while the video was playing was driving me crazy.

The urge for him to touch me grew more and more intense. I just wanted his hands to go under my skirt.

I wanted to feel him slowly while he whispered in my ear that he's not going anywhere. He could come from behind and surprise me, grab my breasts and kiss my neck. I didn't watch porn for a long time. All I needed was his picture. It made me so moist. I'd slide off my panties, wanting him so fucking bad. I loved the fantasies because I was truly in love with him. When I first found out that he had a fiancé, the jealousy burned a strange desire. I would yearn to be his favorite. I'd call him and say "tell me that I'm better than her". "Tell me"! But most of the time when Kanye was dating someone, I'd draw back. I'd protect my feelings and we'd barely talk. I'd second guess if we should try and grow close or maybe just stay on business. I'd still hope for him thou, but I wouldn't date no matter his circumstances. Letting him go seemed more hard to do. I would go straight home and yearn for him nightly. Everything about Kanye turned me on. He was just so sexy to me. I loved the way he dressed. I loved the way he was. I didn't see a flaw in him. Every imperfection was flawless. I believed in him. I saw nothing but the best. I thought there was no wrong in him, like he knew and was everything. I didn't see anything negative about him. Every time I was mad at him or felt that he didn't deserve something, I would convince myself that maybe it was me who was wrong.

You say I think I'm never wrong, you know what, maybe your right. I Wonder, Kanye West

His touch, his kiss, his embrace, I would yearn. I wanted him and him only. For years I wanted no one but Kanye West sexually. There were times when I would become upset with him and sleep with someone else. Then I'd ditch them and go right back into my Kanye West love shell. It was very rare that I slept with anyone and when I did it would be a one night stand and they'd never hear from me again. I enjoyed the thought of wanting Kanye inbetween my legs. I enjoyed the thought of him caressing my body with affection and embrace. I believe it felt right to imagine him in so much excitement, knowing that one day he would finally be really fucking me.

CHAPTER FOUR

"Loving KanYe West with All My Heart"

I was happy to know that Kanye West was single again. "Am I his next girlfriend"? I would wonder. I knew that I wanted to be. Did he know me enough? I thought that he did. I was always posting my feelings for him. He just had to know. Even thou he had many fans, I was sure I was making myself seen. Even thou no one knew how I felt, I knew that he would. I was cocky to believe that I was the only person in the world smart, yet dumb enough to keep my legs closed for him. I felt like celebrity girls had enough money and no patience to wait for him.

Kanye and I talked briefly here and there, but did he think of me as much as I thought of him? The biggest reason why I was always too sure that I'd be with him one day is because of his music and his art. Even thou we rarely spoke, his music is what kept driving me to prove my love to him.

Hood phenomenon, the LeBron of rhyme, Devil in a New Dress

My stage name **Flow** is one of those words that

many rappers use to replace the word **lyrics**. Flow is a slang term used in rap for "what I got to say". However, Kanye had his way of making me feel special.

And I want to show you how you all look like beautiful stars tonight, Runaway, KanYe West

He was with Sumeke Rainey during the recording of his first album, but he made a slick line for Alexis on one of the songs. Don't be stupid to think that it was just a coincidence. Kanye can be smooth, slick and sneaky. To the girl he does it for, it makes you feel so special, trust me I know.

She so precious, with the peer pressure, couldn't afford a car so she named her daughter Alexis, All Falls Down, KanYe West

Well he made the most perfect song for me. The song is called, "Out the game". I honestly heard that song way after we met. My heart was so beating fast when I first heard it. I was like "huh"? I felt so fucking special. I cried, wondering well why can't I touch him then?!

LA face say Linda like Mase but she love face, Out the Game, KanYe West

Ima hit em with the Mase Flow, my, my why should you question me, that she stand next to me, when you the better half of me? Because of You Remix, KanYe West

Throwing shit around, the whole place screwed up, maybe I should call Mase so he can pray for us, Devil in a New Dress, KanYe West

Flow hard as a Chevy, I told her me like ye, she said she like me but when she see me with a C.L like Pete Rock, she just grab the microphone and beat box, My Drink and My Two Step, Cassidy featuring KanYe West and Neyo

She said know what, grow up, you nasty. I don't know why they trippen if ya ask me, Flow just the nicest, Ego, Beyonce featuring Kanye West

Each line has its significance, but I must say that the "My Drink and My Two step" line is my all-time favorite. It says so many things in just one line. Kanye's lyrics were one of the little things he would do that would make me love him. I use to feel no one in the world cared but Yeezy. There are little things he and I know that he did for me and I always loved him for it. I just knew that it was love. The reason I fell for Kanye is because in his own special way he cared. His care made me want more. It made me want all of him. I believe orphans are the main humans wondering who the fuck cares. When someone chooses to care for us, we want to be assured that they really do care. When we know that we know that we know that someone cares, a person like me wants to tell the whole world. Is that wise? Some may not want to speak on their love affairs and for so many reasons it is wise. But there are people who never really had much. When they finally do have, their biggest desire is to boast. For someone to care for me is just as big as me having a record deal! I'd take either. If Kanye was to marry me and tell me not to sing, I was willing to be whatever he wanted me to be. Just love me and it was whatever.

My heart is so devoted. Kanye told me once that I have an addictive personality. I agree. If I like it, I love it. If I fall in love, I fall hard. I'm so funny when it comes to love that I don't want too many people in my circle. When I do be amongst people, I eventually prefer to be alone. But if one person comes in my life and makes me feel special, I'd hold onto them like a fucking magnet. I'd wonder thou, "what if I were getting special attention on the regular, would I cling to it so tight"? Maybe the only reason why I cling to people and things is because real love is hard to find. Maybe it's the way I learned to adapt since childhood. Sitting in the chair waiting and wondering, "who am I going to call mommy next"?" Is it going to be a nice family or a mean one"? "Are they going to love me"? Those thoughts would run thru my head a lot as a child. Once I'd get to a new foster home, if they make me feel like I have something that I didn't have yesterday, I'd pray to God that it wouldn't end. I would begin to call a stranger Mommy, but after doing that so many times it can mess with your nerves.

I guess I cling to people for the sole purpose of never being able to keep everyone that I got close to. It's like a fear of being left alone. I wrote a song in 2007 for Kanye called "Don't Let Me Go". He would always have a girlfriend, but it was beginning to seem like he couldn't keep one. I wrote the song because I knew that I wouldn't want Kanye to let me go. I wanted him to be as much in love with me as I was with him.

"Don't let me go, I'll let you have me if you never ever let me go" Don't Let Me Go"

- Miss Flow

Some people may feel like an orphan grows up and becomes a prostitute or a lost cause. Not everyone is the same. The percentage may be high for that to be the outcome, but some people have things happen during their childhood that keeps them level headed. I don't know what kind of girl I would be without my dad or his family. I still have that orphan personality, but my dad coming in my life gave me a confidence that I didn't have before. After meeting them, thoughts would go thru my head of feeling special and feeling loved. It gave me a new sense of direction. Before they were in my life, I had the thoughts and feelings of hopelessness.

My life was plain boring before. I would just runaway a lot because I felt so unloved in the places I was living. I could always sense neglect and I didn't want to stay anywhere where I felt neglected. Sometimes if I wasn't being neglected, with just a little feeling of it would trigger me to prefer being without them. My dad's family gave me newness.

They weren't assigned by D.C.F.S. and they saved my fucking life! I went from not knowing what to do with my life into having purpose. I created so many ideas, so many dreams and so many hopes from feeling loved by them. What helped the most was when his mom, my grandmother started taking me to church. The pastor made so much sense to me. I went to church when I was smaller and was allowed to sleep during the sermon. I mean, I loved when the choir would sing but I was too little to really understand the message. Going to church with my grandmother at the age 13, the messages taught me a rich way of thinking. I was probably happy that I was a part of something that it made me want to listen. And it made me look at life in a brighter way. Let's not forget Pastor Jackson, who recently retired from pastoring the church I attended. He was one of the best pastors of all time. He put the church first. Before he bought himself a new car or a new house, he paid off the church mortgage. Smart man, don't ya think. He never raised a money dollar offering. It was always just an offering. I hold him in high regard. I loved to listen to his wisdom and how he did things. His mannerism was grand and so was his posture. I watched how he handled things. I loved listening to him speak. He taught me so much. My grandmother who took me to church didn't have her license to keep me in her home. So D.C.F.S eventually moved me to another foster home. That didn't stop me from going to church. I would travel miles away from Chicago Heights to Chicago to attend services. I went often and faithfully. On Wednesday's, Friday's, Saturday's and Sunday's, I'd go out my way to be there. Being around my grandmother made me feel apart of my dad while he was gone in Atlanta. But going to church became a new love. Eventually, I didn't miss him as much anymore.

At the age 26, I was still somewhat clingy. No matter how much church I attended it was still a fear in me of someone letting me go. It was early 2009 and I was watching Kanye West 808's and Heartbreaks on Vh1. I cried. I felt his pain as I stared into the T.V. The entire performance was so intriguing. It was as if Kanye wanted love like me. It was an hour version of his song "Flashing Lights" in my opinion. Dam I loved him so much. I must of passed a millions guys since I met Kanye West, yet he was all that I wanted.

As usual I was doing nothing but searching Kanye on the computer. It was February 22, 2009 when I saw a picture of some white girl on his lap. After hearing rumors of Kanye with this model and that model, I didn't take much to it. Since he left Alexis he was taking pictures with multiple women and kissing them, so seeing this picture meant nothing. Every time Kanye seemed to be dating someone I was always shocked. She wasn't the normal chick that Kanye picked, but there they were standing on the red carpet like a couple. Paris they went and then she's chilling with his crew. Man....I wasn't sad, I was fucking mad!

"Who the fuck was this chick", I was thinking?! This chick is bald headed and dating another woman?! "So this explains the end of his Love Lockdown video huh"?! This explains the line on **"Stronger"** when he said,

"And I'll do anything for a blonde dyke and she'll do anything for the lime light"!

When I saw it, I thought of me. I mean, I liked girls too and I was rocking blonde hair. I even met him wearing blonde hair. In no way did I think he was talking about someone else once again! I felt my devotion at that point was totally in vain. "Kanye how could you"? I was keeping my legs closed for years and even thou we very seldom talked, I would feel his jealousy. I started wishing he stopped. He didn't care enough to tell me to "move on"! I began to hate him at this point. I was willing to understand him dating Alexis, feeling they had history. But after being single and after leaving such a classy woman, this was his choice?! I convinced myself that he was hurting over the death of his mom and over the break-up with Alexis. Maybe he was delusional for a moment. I mean not delusional. Maybe he just wanted to have fun. Why not me thou, ya know?

Kanye and I are both Gemini's. His birthday lands on the 8th of June and mine's is the 13th. In the beginning of June of that year just 5 months later, news hit the fan that Kanye and his current girlfriend Amber Rose had broken up. Yes, I was happy! This was also around the same time that he was going to be doing a concert in our hometown Chicago, on June 10th.

Do you think about me now and then, do you think about me now and then, cause I'm coming home again, Homecoming, KanYe West

This concert felt like heaven. I was happy and it was the best energy ever! He opened up the show performing "Flashing Lights" one of my favorites. "Dam what a beautiful feeling"! I wore a beautiful prom like pink dress, carrying a black purse with some black shoes to match. I was hoping to see him once again. I didn't make much effort that night. I saw G.L.C taking pictures with fans but I didn't want to be a hoe so I said nothing to him. He was in arms reach with no security, but I wanted direct one on one contact with Kanye. I went to the after party that Kanye was quote on quote **"SUPPOSE"** to be at. I'm not a party girl. I go to the club once a year and sometimes not even that, but that's the night I learned that club promoters are full of shit. It was a nice party, but no Kanye. Whatever. I left and didn't let it mess up my night. The moments I had watching Yeezy at his concert stayed on my mind.

Just days later, news broke that Kanye and Amber spent his birthday together. What a fucking waist of hype! But then I thought about it, I knew that if I knew that they were together during his concert, I wouldn't have had so much fun. "Oh well". Unfortunately, I was use to the drama by then.

Months go by and I was starting to feel that they were happy, that maybe he really did love her. Once I finally got that thru my skinny little head, I cried. I remember trying to talk to him and it was as if he didn't want to talk. That made me so fucking sad. I was so dam tired. I felt like I wasted 4 years of my life and I was fucking done with it! I felt stupid and I was so over it!

I grabbed a bottle of ibuprofen and took about 18 pills. I was crying and screaming and I was so fucking sad that I gave all that I could and he didn't love me. How could he not see my worth and keep picking girls who didn't deserve it. I couldn't understand it. I had the signs that he didn't care but I didn't want to believe it because some of the little things he would do showed me different.

My roommate saw me lying on the floor crying next to the bottle of pills. She called the ambulance and I was rushed to the hospital. After that episode, that was it! I no longer wanted to be in love with Kanye! That was my wakeup call! Here I was being overlooked, yet giving my all to Kanye West, a rapper. He was someone miles away who only touched me one time. I needed more than metaphors and lyrics. I needed a touch. I needed a hug and I needed it right now.

Music was always therapy for me, so I went back into the studio to record my first Christmas album. This is something I always wanted to do. When I was younger, every Christmas my foster mom would let me and my sister sit in the living room and listen to Christmas music. Every year I would enjoy listening to the Muffet Babies, Dolly Pardon and other people versions of their Christmas carols. I was excited to be in the studio again. I street performed so much that I rarely went to the studio.

When I finished the Christmas album I decided to sell them at all the churches that I ever attended. With that hustle I was doing well financially. I was moving on from my Kanye West phase. Lonely and willing to date, I was on Black Planet looking for a sexy guy to go out with.

I married at 18, and never really dated. After that I had a two year relationship with my then best friend, Kevin. Outside of that I haven't really enjoyed the dating scene. Most of the time that I didn't date was because I have a habit of isolating myself for whatever reason. I have many reasons I prefer to be alone. When I came out of my shell this time I wondered what was I missing. Most guys on black planet seemed to be losers or not my type. Well, one guy wanted me to chill with him on his birthday. I agreed but I stood his ass up just like I did a lot of guys. But I felt pressured to have some fun the next day when I didn't meet the quota of how many cd's I wanted to sell. I called him up and told him that he could pick me up at the church.

What the fuck was I getting myself into? I was expecting to meet a looser who I could just fuck and never see again. In my mind guys were still nothing if you weren't Kanye. I let him go, but I still felt that guys weren't good enough. I was so use to seeing Kanye spoil his girls and do so much for them. I felt no man but Kanye could make me feel special. So, I didn't think much of these guys.

But Eric, Eric touched me the right way. Eric kissed me the right way. Eric picked me up and fucked me on the wall the right way. He gave me some love making I hadn't had in a fucking long ass time! Dam I wanted more!

He was such a gentleman taking me all the way on the other side of town just to make sure I got home safe. He was a sergeant in the military. A sexy ass 6' foot brown toned sex machine. I fell so head over heels in love with his personality. I loved his touch and care. Being around him made me feel a way that chasing my dreams did not. I felt too scared to go back to me wanting Kanye only. Chasing my dreams seemed so impossible by that point. A door being opened to the industry seemed so far from opened, but a kiss and a hug seemed so near to happening. I threw all my feelings into this guy. I went from being chill and cool to giving him the please don't let me go's. But sooner than later his distance made me wonder and worry. I wanted him to always want to be around me. I know I wanted him inside of me all the time. I wanted to have as much fun as I did with him before.

I started working and stopped street performing. I couldn't concentrate thou. He wouldn't answer my calls. I eventually left the job. Not only was working so new for me, but I was totally distracted by my emotions. I felt I could make easy and fun money singing on Jackson than sitting in that boring ass place. I wanted to cry all day. I started to see that being with him wasn't happening anytime soon. I decided to chase my dreams again and a little harder that time. I made a big move by going to California. I made arrangements to move in with a friend and went to L.A.

L.A was the place to be in March when it's chilly in Chicago. It wasn't as warm as Miami but it'll do. I started street performing in the Promenade and Venice Beach. I was kind of sad not being with Eric. After experiencing love and affection I preferred that than the feeling of chasing something. It felt good to have something right then and there. Chasing my dreams sometimes were boring. The only thing that kept me going was the thought of my dreams coming true one day. But the feeling of signing a contract is probably the same as a man touching my body. I just preferred to be in love. It was one thing when I was accustomed to being alone, but once I felt Eric's touch I just didn't want to let him go.

780

So I decided to do both. I was fucking and singing. It wasn't one night stands. It wasn't just one guy. I was doing the dam thing! In time I wasn't thinking about Eric.

I was sitting on the couch with my friend Charles. He was telling me how Kanye and Amber weren't really happy. He explained to me his opinion that Amber was just with Kanye for money. I didn't want to believe that at that point. I remembered believing that before. I remembered believing that it wasn't real and almost killing myself finding out that it was. I didn't really want to hear that shit!

But sure enough not long after me moving to California was it really true that Kanye and Amber had broken up. "Ah hell naw", I thought! "I am surely about to be the Mrs.", I thought. "No more breaking up with girls, no more chic's over me"! "Kanye was mine"! Shortly after hearing the news about the break-up between Kanye and Amber, news was out that he was having a concert in Chicago. So as soon as I could, I rushed back home. “It was on”, I thought. I wasn’t waiting in my seat with my dress on and legs crossed anymore for him to pick me! I was ready to take what I wanted! I wanted Kanye and I didn’t want no one else to fucking have him, but me!

CHAPTER FIVE

"THE MAKINGS OF MRS. KANYE WEST"

I returned to Chicago with so many ideas rushing through my brain. "I just got to have him"! "I just got to have him", I thought. I was over Eric just that quick. To get Kanye's attention in an artistic way was my plan. I didn't want my feelings to be a secret anymore. I wanted everyone and they mama to know that I was in love with Kanye. I felt it all would work out in my favor. I was an artist craving a record deal and in love with the hottest rapper ever. I may as well put the two together and do the oddest things, both unique and beautiful. Some may see it as me gold digging his money and some may believe that I was just plain crazy. However people was about see it, I knew what place my art was coming from. I knew that I really cared about Kanye West. I didn't know his favorite food, his favorite color or if he preferred lunch or dinner as his favorite meal. But I knew that if Kanye chose me to be his girl, I had enough love in me to care.

I was so focused on Yeezy once again, but it felt

different that time. I felt more in control. I would have totally done things for Kanye right after we met, but he began dating Brooke. Her being in the picture slowed me down. I want to be a princess and feel like a princess. Him picking someone else was like saying, "be a princess somewhere else". I knew so much about Kanye, the rapper. I even kept my legs closed for him for many years. I didn't want my living to be in vain. It felt right for me to go about things this way. I was in a mindset to do the most sexiest and craziest things that would show Kanye and the rest of the world that I was crazy in love with him and talented at the same time. It felt so right. I saw the end of it. I saw me winning his heart. I saw me and him being like Jay and Beyoncé, except were both different from those two. We're nothing mild mannered like those two. That's what makes it so cool. No one needs two of the same. It also wasn't about being like Beyoncé and Jigga and it sure in the hell wasn't competition. It's just that I was in love with a rapper and I sing. The thoughts of me sharing the stage with Kanye took me to higher heights. With every plan that I made, I imagined the end result was

Kanye seeing how much I loved him. I saw him making me his number one. I felt like since he couldn't keep those girls, maybe it would take him being with me to be with someone forever.

I started to create things to show my inner affection for Kanye. I had a website since 2004. The domains would change sometimes but I always had a website outside of social media. I wanted to show all my feelings towards Kanye so I created a website for him. At the 2009 MTV VMA's, Kanye spoke his feelings during Taylor Swift's acceptance speech. He spoke about how Beyoncé should have won the award. There was a certain reaction from people, the kind of reaction that led Kanye to take a step back to evaluate his life. His mother had recently passed a year prior and he never stopped working hard since he started his rise to success in 1999. He was producing, rapping, singing, acting and doing fashion. He was also directing videos and had his own record label. After the reaction from the media, he took a break from interviews and didn't go on the scheduled tour with Lady Gaga. We didn't see much of Kanye in the media for a while. For about 6 months Kanye was quiet to the world. That was until April 2010, when Kanye was releasing new music. He was releasing a new song entitled "Power". Power was the first single from his forthcoming album. It was just the kind of energy I needed with all my feelings and thoughts toward him.

"Got a nice ring to it, I guess every superhero need his theme music" Power

I was so excited to hear from him again in the media. After hearing how some people felt about his behavior at the 2009 Video Music Awards, I named the website, "Kanye Good News". I posted nothing but good things about Kanye. Everything that I posted was positive. There was nothing bad about it. Anything that seemed to be negative, I turned around to put the king on his throne where he belonged. He was a king in my eyes and people should keep that visual of him. Give him a break, I felt. I believed all he needed was love. I felt the chicks that were recently in his life wasn't giving it to him. You have Brooke, who I felt was more about

herself. Then you have Alexis who I assumed was too boogie and too demanding. And last you have Amber Rose who I felt couldn't give Kanye what he was missing. I thought his behavior was because of the lack of real love and support that he needed. He was constantly in the cameras all the time expecting to be the perfect guy. People, the media, and the music industry was yearning energy from Kanye that he didn't have to give. My opinion was that because he was loveless, it had a big effect on his behavior, especially after his mom's passing. I thought I had what Kanye West needed.

I was loveless a lot too, maybe that's why I could sense it so well. I was in so many different foster homes and became close to many people. Growing up I would always find different ways to adapt to my habitat. I did things like changed my last name to my dad's on my school heading. It made me feel like I belonged to him. When I fell in love for the very first time I wrote a note of me and the guys name on my t-shirt. It said "Cedric and Linda 4-ever" with a heart. I always been very loud about who I fell in love with. One thing I noticed thou was that whenever I was truly happy and secure I didn't have to be so loud about who I loved. I think I began to profess my love for people to assure myself and others that the love was still there when it decided to slip away. For everyone that I first met I was always mellow and secure, but there's a part of me that would cling and I would be left standing alone. My feelings would be there and me being loud about my feelings was my way of not letting go.

My dad would be in Atlanta and to keep it from hurting, I would play his recorded tapes around the same time his show would come on. I would claim his last name to still be a part of him. My mother, whom I met at church was different than anyone in my life. She and her husband were the most aggressive lovers that ever walked into my life to this day. They gave me their last name and engraved it in my bible. They knew I lacked love and gave it to me strongly. Their love to this day in my life has been my absolute favorite. I didn't have to claim them, they claimed me. A princess wants to be soft and cuddled. Having parents or a man to give affection to me strongly was the sweetest love I ever known and will ever know. But here I was in love with someone who was too far away to give me a simple hug. Kanye was someone whom I would have stretched a mile just to get a hug from.

After making my blog Kanye Good News, I started performing a lot of Kanye's music. I finally let people know how I felt about him. People on the streets were giving me pet names like "Kanye's wife"," kanYe's girl" or "kanYe's biggest fan". I blushed each time they called me one of those names. I was flattered thinking what I was doing was working. I felt special. I felt a part of Kanye. But one day I took it literally. I was on Jackson Street taking a break, when one of the guys who normally would hang out with me would stick around to protect me. He giggled and said "What's up Ms. Kanye West"? I said "That's it", really loud! I stood on a bench on the subway and said again "That's it"! "My new name is Mrs. Kanye West"! He laughed. I asked him ""Do you think I'm joking"? He laughed again and said "no I believe your very for real". I laughed, smiled and said, "Watch this"!

Sure enough I changed my website from Miss Flow.com to Mrskanyewest.com. People were familiar with the name Miss Flow. After having that name for 6 years I wasn't sure how people would react to my new stage name. I didn't know just how it would grow on people. I was curious but I didn't too much care either. I was so excited to wear that name. I felt closer and more connected to Kanye using his name as my name. He was still single and I kept having an adreniline rush, hoping that he did not start dating someone. I would always be in a rush to do the unthinkable. I would make it known that I was Kanye's number one fan. I felt like I'm the one Kanye needed to end up being with and not anyone else. I wanted to do things like Kanye in some ways, but not copycat him. I wanted it to be about how much I liked him. I wasn't trying to be the next him. I in no way wanted to cop Kanye style or try to be better than him. I would have never used his name as an artist just for attention.

Mrs
Kanye
West
.com

The only attention I wanted was Kanye's. I was so devoted. I wanted when Kanye finally fucked me, my pussy would be tight. That was one of the things I tried to impress him with, my tight pussy. I know he liked that too.

Ahhh put a pussy in a sarcophagus, Monster, KanYe West

Why I only got a problem when you in the hood, the only thing I wish, I wish a nigga would, Good Life, KanYe West

I had my reasons of doing things as an artist who was in love with Kanye. I started wearing nothing but pink because of the issues that came about when Kanye's was wearing pink. People didn't think he should have worn pink because he's a man. Umm, I saw my step-dad wear a pink suit on many occasions. My pastor wore pink and purple suits. In other words, wearing pink was my way of sticking by Kanye. It looked good on me too. I fell in love with pink. The change was starting to grow on people quick. I heard chuckles when I announced my website, but in the back of my mind I would think, "hmm watch how you won't be laughing one day". I knew I was too smart for my own good. I knew that if I was special enough for Kanye to rap about me, I knew that it was also possible to be with him one day. How was still the question. I wasn't too worried thou because the ball was in my court now. I knew I was bold enough to do anything for his love.

I started rocking a teddy bear in my pink book bag and wore watches like he did. I ordered tons of t-shirts with my website on it. The image was clear that I was a Kanye fanatic. I did things Kanye would do and wore things that represented him. I was feeling myself. I felt more apart of him. I felt like this was a start of what I was hoping for. I started to believe that waiting on Kanye may not have been in vain after all.

I got to thinking more and more about what I was going to do next. Wondering what to do and what say to show that I loved Kanye. I wanted to be loud enough for the world to hear me. I wasn't going to be overlooked anymore, PERIOD! I felt that way about Kanye and my career. I'm saying, even thou people

99

100

use Kanye West name on YouTube to get views for their video, but I had a legitimate reason for using it. It was until after I decided to use his name that I realized how much attention it would get. I wasn't trying to be the next Kanye West. Even thou we do think and act alike, I wasn't trying to be him. I was doing what I have done my entire life. If I loved someone, I'd let that show in ways that made me feel secure. I would boast. I would brag. I would change my name on my school paper. I would talk about them all the time. I would excessively love something they gave me or bond with something that reminded me of them. I just did a lot of adapting to a lot of different people that I came to love my whole life.

After changing my stage name and getting people to finally know just how crazy I was for Kanye West, I went into the studio to make music about him. I was overly excited about making my first album. I wanted to do it the Kanye West way. I wanted to produce the music. Since I produced songs before, I felt I could produce an entire album, and I did. The songs that weren't produced by me were Kanye tracks. I put my own flavor to his songs "Flashing Lights", "Crack Music", and a beat that he made for Jay-Z called "Girls, Girls, Girls". The title that I gave my songs were "Dear Kanye, Never Gonna Let You Go, I'm Mrs. Kanye West, Virgin To My Love, Open My Heart Again and This Man's Heart". And that's just to name a few. The lyrics covered my feelings from the past 5 years that I loved and waited for him. I was feeling the music and so were a lot of people. It had a 90's feel to it by the drum beats, rhythm, and melody. And even thou I put my music on I-tunes, I wanted to do more with it.

It was like the more and more I did, the more I felt I was going to really be Mrs. Kanye West one day. I was doing things that made me feel more and more apart of him. My name and image started to grow on people. I could tell how the people who were familiar with my hip-hop an r&b style saw another side of me that they didn't know exist. I went from wearing jeans and dressy shirts to wearing masks and doing things that only is truly understood in the pop culture.

Since my album was complete I was ready to do something with it. Nothing I was doing I wanted to be normal. I wanted to stand out in every way, as I have my whole life. I do believe most people that want to stand out are lacking internal affection, but it is what it is and it was what it was. Either way those people exist and are out here. Life would be boring without the excitement of all kinds of personalities. So, yea I do like it when I'm content, in love, assured and quiet, but I felt I was doing what I had to do. On top of that it was becoming fun. I was always full of excitement doing everything that I was doing.

I decided to take my music to New York and sell it. Singing my song and promoting my cd in the barber shops seemed to be the best plan. I've hustled the barber shops before in Chicago and thought it would be pretty cool to do it in New York. I arrived in New York, July 2010 for the third time. The first time was to see Kanye West perform and the second time I thought I could live in New York, but only stayed a little while.

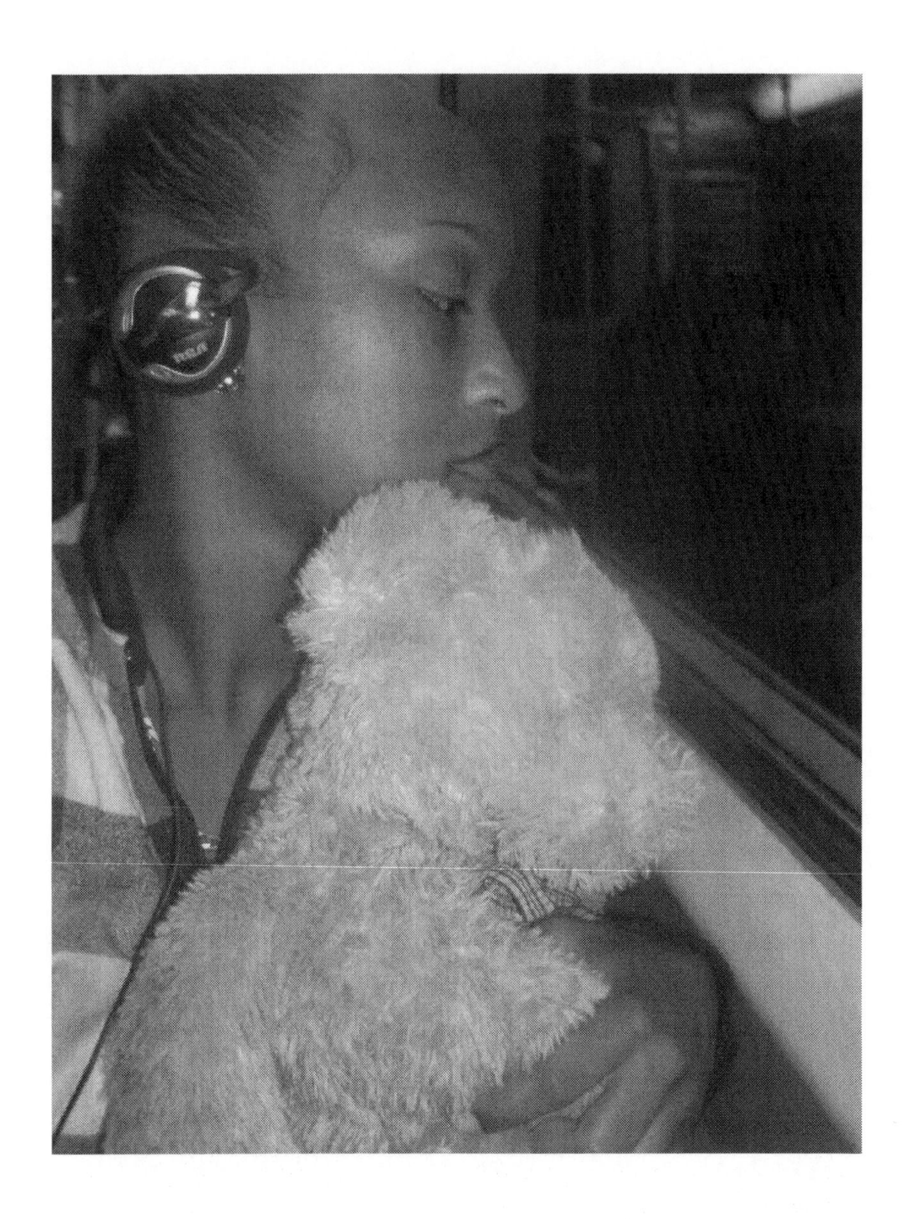

I began doing things I never did before but always had the energy to do. If it wasn't for him having girlfriends left to right, I would have been let out my crazy ideas.

I'm head of my time, sometimes years out, but the powers that be won't let me get my advance out Gone, Kanye West

To sell my cd in the barber shops, my plan was every Friday and Saturday to go through all the boroughs. The boroughs are split up in 4's. You got Brooklyn, the Bronx, Manhattan, and Queens. Harlem is just a section located in Manhattan. I felt like I was building a resume with my talent doing those different things. I felt the more I gave Kanye his props, one day he would give me mine.

Many people were against the whole Mrs. Kanye West name, but seeing my cd, my t-shirt and teddy bear, they couldn't help but go along with it. And if they still weren't feeling it, I wouldn't give a dam and I'd tell them that too. I'm very firm about something that I believe in and could give ten fucks about how someone disagrees. If it's in my heart let it be and worry about yours, cause I gone get mine.

Every weekend I sold about 20-40 cd's for $10. I was making about $200-$400. I was ordering costumes, taking care of bills, and getting things that I needed with the money. I was having fun with the people who had a lot of questions about my feelings for Kanye. I loved every minute answering those questions too. I knew that I was the only one bold enough to go this hard. Women may have loved Kanye the same, but I was more than ready to outshine them hoes.

Ideas were constantly coming to me about being Mrs. Kanye West. I wanted to be more like the name itself. So, since my name was Mrs. Kanye West, why not I dress like a bride? Even thou I was already keeping my legs closed, I wanted to be more out there with how I felt. I wanted what I felt on the inside to show. I was rocking the teddy bear and the pink, but I wanted to be a little more extreme. So, I decided to be a bride. I ordered the cheapest yet prettiest gloves and veil from ebay.com. And I picked out the prettiest white dress from Cookies. Cookies is a popular store downtown, Brooklyn.

After getting my wedding dress look together, "I was about to be doing it best", I thought. I was prepared to look so pretty and make Kanye so proud. In time I made all the money that I needed to make in order for me to sing at my dream place, Times Square. As a street performer, you really want a record deal like most musicians. A musician wants enough money to pay for their own equipment and expenses easy. A street performer can make a good penny, but it feels good to have limos and a big house that you dream of as a kid. I dreamed of singing on big stages, but since I haven't had the chance to, singing in Times Square was close enough to it. Times Square is located in Manhattan, New York. It's full of beautiful lights and stores. People tour it 24 hours a day. The beautiful thing about Times Square to me is the colorful lights and images. I also love how it's always full of people. That is my favorite place to sing.

There I was in a white wedding dress so happy. I felt everything that I did in the last couple months was for that moment. I looked and felt beautiful.

As I was taking a break from performing the very first day I sang in in Times Square, I started looking through my phone when I saw a picture of Kanye and Selita Ebanks together. He was promoting this film called “Runaway” with her. But “why the fuck is he holding hands with her”, I thought. “What the fuck”!? “This is my day”, I felt. I didn’t want to lose. I’ve come too far. I couldn’t loose. All this time he wasn’t with any girl, and the day I decide to sing in my wedding dress, he pull this off!? He knew it too! He knew my whole agenda that entire summer. I went home mad and got on the computer. I watched his video “Coldest Winter” and cried till I couldn’t cry no more. “He knows I was doing this for him, why is he continuing to be a fucking douche bag,” I thought! Man, only God knows how I felt. I in no way saw that coming. I wanted to be his queen. After doing all of that, shouldn’t I have been crowned?

Couldn't he see how much I loved him? But I wasn't going to stop there! I had come too far at that point. It was on!!!!!!!!!

CHAPTER SIX

“GIVING MY ALL TO KANYE”

It was easy to love Kanye while being quiet about it because I could bounce back in between feelings. But it was another thing when his name was tattooed on my arm. It was different when two big cities knew me as "Mrs. Kanye West". I guess I felt like a true celebrity for once in my life. I had to figure out how to fix my image because of what people knew. He was single when I began this journey, but was he single now? This would affect me as an artist and it would break my heart if Kanye was really dating Selita Ebanks. It wasn't known yet if they were truly dating or not. So far, they were just rumors.

For the first time, I believed it. This was the first time I wasn't in doughts about who Kanye West chose to date. At that point I was like shit you never know with Kanye. He kept picking woman that weren't up to standards seemed like. In my opinion Kanye could have picked woman who had something going for themselves other than girls that just looked good. And when I finally did believe that he'd date such a girl, it wasn't even true. The news was that they weren't official. From all the pictures of them holding hands, being lovey dubby, she can keep that "we didn't even kiss bullshit" for someone who believe that. She could have kept that shit straight to herself. Aint nobody believing that but you, chic. She kissed my man. That's right; I said it, "my man"!

I still began to notice that he was picking woman who weren't keeping their legs closed and woman who dated a lot of men in the course of a year. As I realized that I wasn't even trying to impress him with my good girl ways. I was more so just trying to get my point across. I was drawn into the media hype. If Kanye saw my value and worth then maybe I'd care again. I was nonchalant about things because I started to feel like my love was in vain. I felt like even after doing all of that I had done I was being overlooked. My feelings took a turn. I started to have this get rich or die trying feeling. Kanye knew exactly what I was doing and how I felt. Kanye could have at any point snapped me into reality and he didn't. He was very quiet about how he felt. I think the more that I didn't know the more that I kept trying. I felt empty. Since I had already promoted this image of being a Kanye Fanatic I decided to keep going. But I wanted to say "Fuck this bullshit"! I went from being the girl in a wedding dress to this wild chic who demanded Yeezy's love. I started putting films on local TV about my feelings for Kanye but they were a bit dramatic.

When I was young I wrote a play, a book and hosted many programs for the teens in my community. I did them out of boredom. I felt important like I was doing something. I felt worth something. I felt like a leader. I grew a lot of respect for the things that I would do. People were always impressed with how I had such a talent. I would write the book, print the book, and put the book together. I would write the play, direct the play, invite everyone to the play, and so on. I would always want to have complete control, fearing someone wouldn't do it like I liked. And it would all turn out well just like I wanted. So when I started putting together tv films, it was right up my lane.

My first show was very interesting. I did a lot of fun and exciting things that brought out a lot of humor. I dressed up as Kanye while performing his song "Heartless". I would mocked him out of humor. I performed some songs in a wedding dress on the subway telling him how I felt. The real humor came on when I appeared to be yelling at Kanye on camera about holding Selita Ebanks hand. From there I wanted to do so much more and I did. Every show had its involvement with whatever Kanye was doing at the time. I would focus on how I felt about it. To be honest it just seemed like I was more and more mad at him on each film. I would pretend to be on the phone with him and upset that he wasn't holding me. In the end, it was made to be funny even thou a part of me really did feel like the angry character I was portraying. It was still made for people to laugh. My show would come across the screen as "Mrs. Kanye West" and grew a great following.

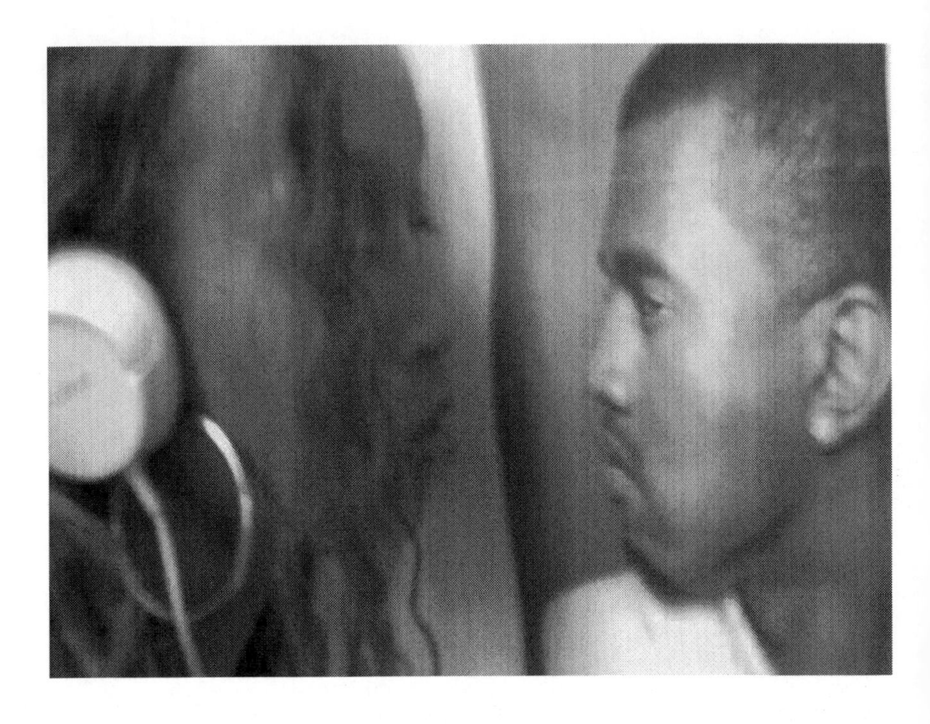

From all the noticeable things that led people to know that I was in love with Kanye West, everyone did not agree with my name change. Some people would tell me that because it was Kanye's name I shouldn't use it. Oh really?!

I told you once before that I could give a good dam about people's opinions. It was like living in a foster home and someone telling me that I wasn't blood related to them. Okay then, let's go make this shit official then. Umm, how do I do that? Well, fuck my real name! I didn't like the piece of shit in the first place. Linda was cool but the rest could go anyways.

There I was April 29, 2011 in front of a judge changing my legal name. It was Linda Resa and that day it became Kanyeresa. That felt much better! Now what they got to say?! Oh nan na, what's my name?! I must have laughed the entire time that I was doing it thinking, "Am I really doing this shit?" But that's my ego. Don't tell me I can't do something. In my mind I can do whatever the fuck I want to do. Long

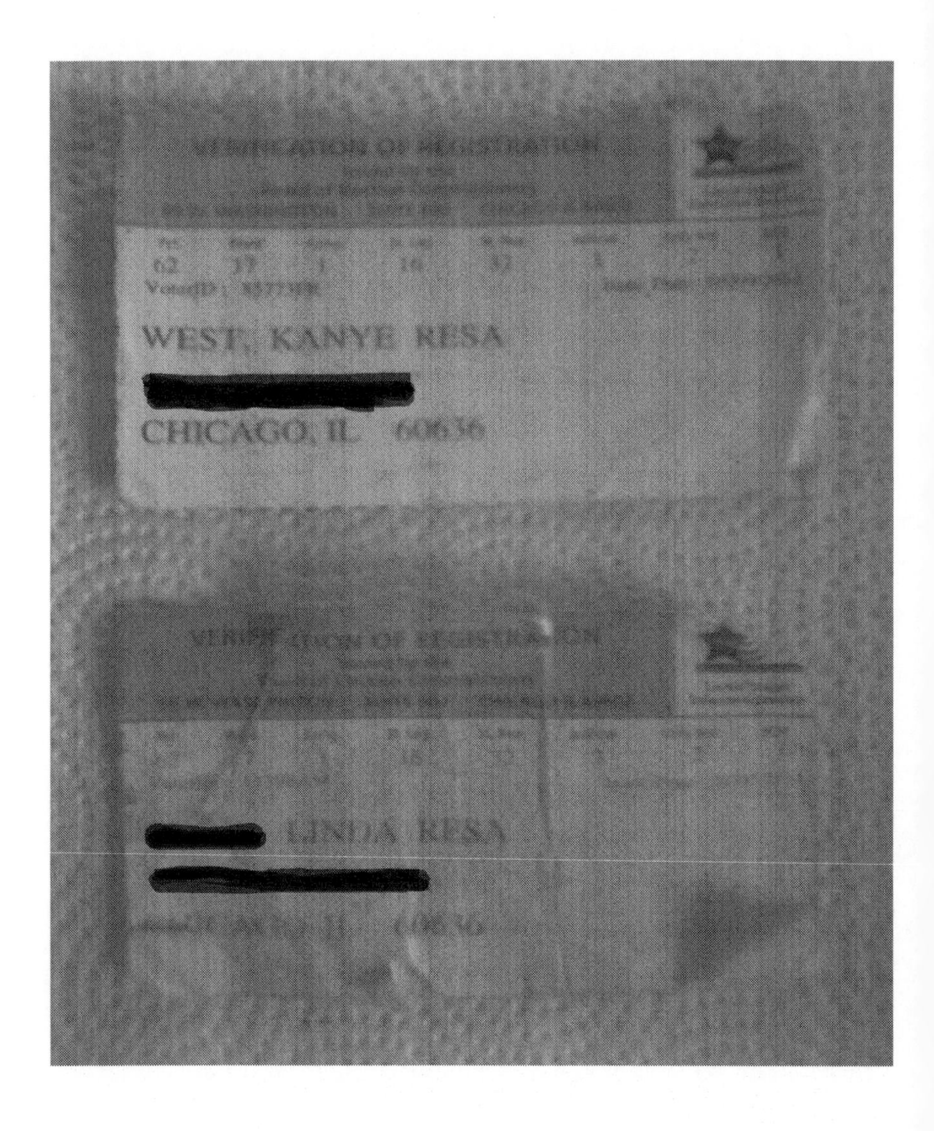

VERIFICATION OF REGISTRATION

62 17 1 16 32 5

WEST, KANYE RESA

CHICAGO, IL 60636

VERIFICATION OF REGISTRATION

LINDA RESA

60636

as I'm not hurting anybody, why should it be no to you? Let me do me and you fucking do you. Now that Kanye's name was on my state ID, I swear I felt better. I was waiting to hear somebody say something so I could be like "you can't tell me nothing"! Seemed like I never had a problem after that. "Aint that bout some shit", I would think. Oh well, it was truly official then. I was really a part of Kanyeezy. My name was Kanyeresa West at the bank, at the aid office, at school, as a street performer and so on. It was my name now, so shut the fuck up is how I felt! Summer, 2011 I wanted to try and perform at New York Times Square again. I felt like I never knew what could come from singing on the streets of New York.

Tuesday
Tuesday
Tuesday

Four months straight I performed cover tunes in a wedding dress and sometimes pink dresses in Times Square. I would rock the crowd, giving my all. I expected the best whether it was Kanye walking up behind me and surprising me or whether it was a contract. I won't lie I expected some kind of honor for loving yeezy so hard. I had always expected the best outcome. I went to 106th and Park. Rosci gave me my props and I appreciate her for that. Yea, I felt special I admit it. But I deserved that and more, I felt. I went to 106th and Park the exact day Kanye and Jay Z's "Watch the Throne album was released. Dam that cd was hot and so was that day. I turned my radio on as I was on my way to purchase my copy of the cd. Hot 97 was banging the whole album non-stop. Flex was playing "No Church in The Wild" as soon as I turned my radio on. Dam what a great feeling! I left New York at the end of Summer, 2011 and headed back to Chicago, me and Yeezy's hometown.

CHAPTER SEVEN

"KANYE WEST GIRLFRIENDS"

I remember finding out about Brooke, the first girlfriend Kanye went public with. Everyone knew about Sumeke Rainey who was his girlfriend from Chicago, but he never really exposed her. He talked about her in a couple of songs, had a couple of pictures with her, but that's about it. We didn't know much about him and Sumeke like we knew about the others he would date. I cried a lot thou when I heard about Brooke. When you first meet someone there is less anger. They haven't let you down a lot so it's easy to keep giving them a try, so I didn't give up when I found about Brooke. I felt I could deal with anything to win Kanye's heart. I mean who was I? I had just met him. I mean I was just a fan. I was lucky to even be talking to him. How could I be mad? I always felt that Kanye was right and I just had to work hard to get him. When he was with Brooke I remember the 2005, Zingle Ball Bash. I could almost sense them trying to reconcile differences. The look in their eyes were as if he was trying to reassure her something. And she gave off this "I'm trying to trust you vibe". It looked couple cute. It appeared to me that none of his relationships would ever fail. I was so sure that each and every last one of his relationships had something too special to let go. I even felt that way about his ex, Amber Rose. When I found out about Alexis Phifer being engaged to Kanye West, I was shocked. I couldn't believe it. I just didn't see why me and Kanye wasn't hooking up. All the time I invested in him made me always question myself when I would see him holding another girls hand. I'd think to myself, Yeezy how could you be so heartless?

How could you be so cold as the winter wind when it breeze yo, Heartless

Amber and Kanye actually looked cute togather. I even got use to seeing Brooke. She and Alexis seemed like the perfect rappers wife. I assumed that it would last forever. But it didn't. I would wonder why. Was she too prissy? Was she too beautiful? Was he just too much of a cheater? I always wondered the reasons behind his break-ups. The media never really gave too much detail of why his relationships would end, we just knew that they did.

Kanye was the kind of guy who would brag on a girl. He would assure the world that the girl that he was dating was the one. He'd give that assurance through songs, videos, and interviews. So why did the relationships end? What was he hiding?

Kanye is a very popular rapper, his image is important to him, and so is his business. One of the reasons why he is so private about his personal life is so that he can protect it and be the best rapper that he can be. What does his relationship business have to do with people anyway? They were interested in him because of his music, not his dick size. Even if they were just interested in his dick size, I'm sure Kanye didn't need to announce to the whole world his relationship problems. Dealing with the media and their opinions about his music was enough. Unless he expressed it through this music, he wouldn't give a lot of information about his love life.

When he was dating Alexis I was focused on Getting Out My Dreams. I wanted to be apart of Kanye West's label, G.o.o.d Music. I wanted to be the first lady. "At least give me that since it was obvious I couldn't have his heart". When they were dating I continued to sing on Jackson Street without pursueing my career. I wasn't auditioning for anything. I just expected Kanye to eventually be there. I look back and think about how that was the best time to pursue my dreams. I was only 24 and 25 years old. That would have been the best age for me to break into the music industry. Well somehow I thought Kanye was going to fall out the sky and sign me. I learned in time that chasing a dream means just that. It means to go after, pursue, and strive to be the best in all that you believe.

There are celebrities who have family members with undiscovered talent. So my dream wasn't going to fall out the sky just because of who I knew. Instead of me believing that talking to Kanye meant that he was just going to hand me a deal, I should've worked hard trying to get one. I slowed down so much when it came to performing and perfecting my craft. I could have taken piano lessons and learned how to play better. I could have auditioned for Broadway. I could have done so many things but instead I depended on Kanye West for my dreams.

I learned that putting yourself first is something that you MUST do. Sometimes no one will tell you that and sometimes they will. Sometimes you may not understand why you should put yourself first, but it is very important to know that you are in control of yourself. No one can do a better job at making decisions for you, like you. No one knows what is best for you and what will make you happy, like you. No matter how convincing their words over your life are, no one can see it like you can. Everyone sees different and feels different about life. If I would have thought for myself and not allowed someone else to think for me, I would have had the best time of my life in my 20's.

But there I was 25, single and still crazy about Kanye West. In 2008, right before his Glow In The Dark

Tour he became single. Of course I was shocked he called off his engagement with Alexis. Their pictures together were so beautiful and she started to seem like the perfect bride. She didn't seem like a fame whore and appeared very classy. "What was wrong now", I thought. But you know I was happy, just surprised. Despite how curious I was of the why's and why not's, I honestly just wanted to be sure it was really over.

Even thou Kanye and I talked, I didn't know where he lived or what his next move would be. I didn't spend a lot of time talking to him because I was more interested in seeing him. How was I going to see him thou? I was waiting for him to say, "Come on lets go".

I believed it was possible for me and Kanye to be together after finding out how he starting dating Alexis. He got to know her as a friend while he was dating Brooke. I imagined this could be the same outcome with me and him. We weren't sleeping together and I was being a good girl for him. It only felt right. I didn't think any other girl was going out of their way for Kanye as I was. I'm sure he had model chicks sucking and riding the shit out of his dick on a daily basis, but I couldn't fanthom other woman sheltering their lives for Kanye like I was. I felt I was making the ultimate sacrifice. I didn't know where Kanye lived or what kind of car he drived. I wasn't aware of how we could meet, I was just sure that it was going to happen one day.

I remember hearing Amber on a radio interview talking about how she liked girls and boys. I saw pictures of her bangin body and was thinking Kanye can't be serious about this chic. Kanye West is dating her? My Kanye West? The gentleman who doesn't have a lot of tattoos or peircings is now dating a stripper. At that point, I was like yea, Kanye is full of surprises. I never expected that. He started dressing different, not to mention the way she dressed was like "woah"! I was wondering was he just doing this because he was going through so much or did he really like this girl? Eventually I convinced myself that the rock star life was changing Kanye. His music was even different. At first it was soulful, but his music started to sound contemporary and pop. I didn't think it was a bad thing that he was changing. I'm aware that as time changes, people do too. I was also aware that Kanye had gone through a lot. It just had to grow on me. I was use to the other Kanye, but I stayed in love with him anyway.

Living in a different world and not in a hard knock situation can cause you to breathe easier. He was chill in my opinion and just wanted to try different things. But after Kanye left Amber Rose I wanted to be next! Fuck next, I should have been first! It was time for me to be with my man!

They be on the internet but they never cop nothing

Number One, John Legend featuring Kanye West

CHAPTER EIGHT

"WATCH THE THRONE"

One thing that inspired me was the "Watch The Throne" album. I started to feel like what I was doing for Kanye was in vain, but that album made me second guess giving the fuck up. I mean every time Kanye released something I was hyped. This was no different. I even liked some of Jay –Z joints but had no idea that the album was that fucking hot! The beats were so fucking soulful. It was like "The College Drop-Out" combined with "The Blue-Print". It was fucking hot yo! The lyrics made you feel like you could do anything. This collaboration was the best collaboration of all time in my lifetime, period! These two ego maniacs together sent out a message that simply said "fuck garbage and love life". The thing that I love about the album is that they opened up on some real shit about themselves.

As men, they poured out their heart. Sometimes they came off arrogant and sometimes they came off humble. Either way anyone could that tell it was genuine.

"Who Gon Stop Me" is my favorite song from Jay-Z. Even thou I love all the songs, I must say that I became a Jay-Z fan after hearing that song.

Shit got to come in some way, when you growing up worthless. Middle finger to my old life, graduated from the corner, street smart and I'm book smart Jay-Z, Who Gon Stop Me

I must admit thugs would never catch my attention. I wouldn't pay attention to a guy who represented himself as a thug, let alone listen to his music. Unless it was on the radio, I wouldn't pay it no mind. I always had mad respect for Jay for signing Yeezy, but I only heard his music on the radio. After hearing "Watch The Throne" I started to listen to all of Jay-Z's music. I purchased the "Blue-Print" album, "Kingdom Come", "The Black Album", "Reasonable Dought" and his album "American Gangsta". I started to learn that Jay-Z's path was similar to my present. He talked a lot about standing on the corners trying to make a living. I don't agree with drug dealing or drug using because I see what It does to people and I don't like it, but I respect Jay-Z for changing his vision. He started making money selling cd's on the street corners, turned around and built an empire. His so called pipe dream turned into a lot of money.

That same man built a label that he and his partner Dame Dash started, Rocafella Records. That same label is also the only label that believed in Kanye West. Jay and Dame are the type of guys who are hard-core and very stern. They can be brutal if you cross them are the same ones who believed in Kanye West when no one else did. I started to never judge a book by its cover.

The reason why I started to respect Jay-Z music so much is because he took his money and turned it into being not only a famous rapper, but one of the smartest business men in our time. He's the black Donald Trump, except smarter in my opinion. I would hear a lot about Jay –Z because he's married to Beyoncé. I have been a Beyoncé fan since the beginning of her career. You won't catch me talking bad about her because you'd be dumb not to respect her. I don't know about her personal life, but what I do know is that she is a great entertainer. She releases music and performs in ways that you can't help but love. I'm not a hater. Yes I wanted to be at Beyoncé status when I was little. I wanted to be the hottest chic in the game. But I confess Beyoncé does a great job at being hot. One thing I love about her and Jay is not only are they great performers, but I have always admired their relationship. They make the black community more than they may know feel like there is fucking hope. All people really want to do is be in love and know that someone won't leave them. Their music and appearances together give us that. If it wasn't for Jay & Beyoncé and Will & Jada we wouldn't feel no hope of love. The industry is always announcing these amazing couples uniting and just months later the relationships fails.

Most celebrities that people look up to, do what feels right. Well, feelings always change and the example that they set appears to the world that it's okay to make a big commitment and just leave. But it's not okay. The world would be a better place if we could just keep family. My feelings changed about Kanye over the course of 7 years. I wasn't even getting what his girlfriends would get from him. But despite feelings that are fickle and are bound to change, I had a ride or die heart.

I'm sure Beyoncé and Jay-Z have come to so many brick walls, but they stay together. What I also love is that you don't see pictures of Beyoncé kissing other men and you don't see pictures of Jay-Z kissing other women. You may hear a rumor and it could be, but that's about it. Whether the rumors are true or not, I respect the way that they have handle things over the years. People who do things for the camera do to be seen and the only thing we get out of it is people reactions. But when you are true to yourself and are truly in love with someone, you'd know how to value and keep it.

So this album was what kept me from giving up on loving Kanye West. I should have let go. I should have been let go of this fantasy. It wasn't like I was married to Kanye. No one in my family agreed with me when it came to my feelings for Kanye. But my mom always understood and stood by me regardless. My dad was beginning to understand me too. Since Kanye was still single I couldn't help but to do more for the chance of being his Beyoncé. Yes there is only one Beyoncé, but you get what I mean.

December 1st was the concert to fucking remember. The only person I seen in concert as an adult was Kanye West, but that was about to change. Kanye West and Jay-Z was in all black. It was so much fucking fun. I started listening to Jay-Z's music so I knew a lot of his songs during the show. When both of them gave each other the stage to perform their own songs, I was in tuned with both of them. It was so much fun, and people were so hyped. The best part of the night that hyped me so much was the feelings that I had for Kanye.

I enjoyed his "Runaway" performance. I saw it on YouTube from their previous shows in other cities, but it was more amazing to see it live. The last song they performed together was **"Niggas In Paris".** When they finished the song, everyone would walk to the door, expecting the concert to be over. And l didn't want to leave. They didn't want to leave. I felt like I could look at Kanye's face all night and trust me I wanted to.

WTF! The music started again. Everyone was fucking crunk and happy! We would all run back to our fucking seats with our hands in the air, "like yea"! And this happened at least 9 times. The adrenaline rush that they gave us never knowing when they would stop the show was by far the best anxiety ever! Let's not forget that I showed up in a wedding dress.

She said Ye can we get married at the mall? I said look you need to crawl fo' you ball

Niggas In Paris, KanYe West

CHAPTER NINE

"THE MEDIA"

I guess I wasn't over Kanye like I thought I was. Deep down I felt as long as he was single, I would keep coming up with new ideas to impress him. In 2010, I got my first tattoo on my arm that says; "KanYe" with a heart in place of the "a". I didn't want a tattoo growing up because I had disbeliefs about them. I never thought it was sexy getting ink or piercings on the body. But the further I went out my way to impress Kanye, the more I agreed doing the unthinkable. I remember how it felt getting my first tattoo. I felt that if nothing said I liked Kanye, getting his name on me would. I just knew I would mean a lot to him after doing something like that. Right after I got the arm tattoo I wanted to get his name on my ass. It wasn't until after I went to the "Watch the Throne" concert that I decided to get it.

Since I started my blog "Kanye Good News" in 2010 I went back to my Kanye West love shell. I wasn't having sex and I wasn't dating. Once again I didn't want to have sex with anyone but Kanye. And being celibate for him made it easy for me to want his name big and bold on my ass. It wasn't a big ass deal to me to get his name on my ass. I believed so deeply that I would end up being Kanye West girl one day, so I got his name tattooed big and bold across my ass. I loved it. I love my tattoo. I felt I was so much closer to winning all of his heart after doing that. I thought to myself "this some ride or die shit right here". I felt like the baddest chic of 'em all.

By the end of 2011, I made a lot of big statements on how much I cared for Kanye West. In my eyes the tattoo on my ass had to be the biggest statement of all. Not knowing much about the media other than not to fully trust their words, I found out something. When the news about my tattoo went viral everywhere online the next day it shocked me, but amazing at the same time. I was so hyped. I was happy to hear many people give me the respect I felt I deserved. They called me crazy but I didn't mind it. I kind of agreed. Yes I was crazy for going as far as I did for Kanye. Now crown me his crazy queen!

In my opinion when people call me crazy it's a definition for unique, out the box, and out of the ordinary. So thank you, because I never ever wanted to be like everyone else. I always wanted to be treated special and I always wanted to be special. Everyone's dream is to shine. Whether someone wants to sing or be a lawyer, we all want to be the best of the best. No one wants to be overlooked. Most of the time when you're happy in a relationship you don't need the worlds approval. When a person makes you feel crowned like a king or a queen, that is all you need. But when you lack simple affection like me that's when you look elsewhere. I admit I wanted it all with Kanye. I wanted the ring, the deal, the house and the kids.

I was quite amazed by the exposure I was getting. I was also quite amazed that people were all excited over my big ass tattoo. People were able to go to my website and see that this crush was more than an attention moment. I was actually living this fantasy. I had a "Beautiful Dark Twisted Fantasy" to be Kanye's girl and to be Kanye's wife.

FM

One day on Jackson Street I received an email. I was very surprised when I saw who it was that was emailing me. It was the love of my life, Kanye West. Every time before that time I was the one who would start the conversation. It had been a long time since we talked and we had only talked here and there. He started an argument with me and in no way did I take it serious. The first reason I didn't take it serious was because of the fact that he contacted me. The second reason was it didn't fucking matter.

I was talking to him and that meant more to me than anything. I was as nice as I could be because I wanted him to calm the fuck down so he could tell me something sweet. Sure enough he did. It was February 2012 and Kanye was in London working on his fashion line. We started talking all the time about everything. One thing I was so happy about is that he was willing to open up to me. We weren't having conversations where I was just talking about me. He was talking about himself as well. He shared his feelings about his fashion line and how hard he was working. He compared the people who criticized his fashion line to the people that I deal with on the subway. He wanted me to know that it wasn't easy for him either, but that we could make it. I wasn't tripping that Kanye didn't send me a check. I was on my grind and he was on his. Eventually I felt things would happen, but I would never sweat it.

When we talked before we were mostly talking about me. I assumed that he was more into me than before because he started to share more about himself. I was falling more in love except this time I had a connection with Kanye. I felt maybe he feels the same way that I do. I decided to go back to school. Every day during class Kanye was distracting me. He would send me instant messages and I couldn't help but respond to him. Late at night I'd be so tired from a long day and yet would wake up and chat with him. Barely woke, but I'd always answer for my baby.

You know what I was thinking right? I was thinking that this was it. I was thinking that I finally have the chance to be with my baby. I felt like, "It worked"! If you believe in something you can have whatever it is that you want. I was on cloud 9.

I would imagine him flying me to Paris and London. I would imagine us making love. I would imagine me being the girl sitting next to him in one of those boring ass Fashion Show seats. I knew best not to share that me and him were talking. As always I respected his wishes. He does not like people in his business and I can understand that.

He told me one day that he was preparing a contract. I asked him, "for who"? He said, "me". I replied calm but in the back of my head, I was like "OMFG REALLY"! Kanye wasn't just my favorite, but in my eyes he was the world's favorite. Kanye signing me to his label meant the world to me. I been in fantasy zone for 7 years imagining Kanye in my world and for it to come true brought me to grateful tears. I was so fucking happy. But I just replied to him, "cool". He promised to see me when he got the states. I was so ready for all of this to happen. I felt like I bent over backwards just for those moments and I was so fucking happy that they were finally there.

So what the fuck was this news about him and Kim Kardashian? I was mad that he was even in the fucking paper with her, but I didn't get too worked up because it was just Kim Kardashian.

CHAPTER TEN

"KIMYE"

Here I was once again in denial. After seeing Kanye pick so many different kinds of woman, I was truly in denial about this one. But see this was not the first time Kim Kardashian has been rumored dating Kanye, so I overlooked it. I was also in denial because I was so sure that Kanye's next girlfriend would be his wife. I didn't see Kanye taking Kim serious with a past like hers. She dated so many men and I didn't see anything serious about her so I didn't think that he would take her serious. When I finally believed that Kanye was dating Selita E-Banks, he really wasn't. I thought maybe I was right again.

Oh shit! Another picture was posted and then it was another. I questioned him about it and he said that he was just trying the friendship out to see where it would go. A week later Kim denied having a relationship with Kanye as well on tv. She claimed that they were just friends. I was real happy to hear that. I was thinking, "Okay so now stop seeing the bitch". I wouldn't tell him that thou. Kanye would constantly say to me that he wanted me instead of her. Yet on Google it said different. The lies made me fucking furious. I threw everything in my room and started packing. Where the fuck was I going I did not know. I was so upset that he would do this to me again! Except that time that we talked we were having more intimate conversations. I had a reason to believe that he was feeling me. I was sad. I was mad and I was angry. The real big ticker was when Kim Kardashian was on "The Friday Night Project".

"The Friday Night Project" is a show that airs in the U.K. She was asked what was up with her stupid earrings that said "KW". Her response was that "since I don't believe in getting tattoos, the earrings were the best way to show affection for my man". Her man?! What?!

GOT
99
PROBLEMS
KIM K.
AINT
ONE!

I didn't know if I should have been mad at the fact that she indirectly said my tattoos were nothing or the fact that I had just heard that their relationship was official. Either way I was mad. Kanye's name was on my ass, arm, and my breasts. I was thinking "what the fuck do I do now"?! Past the emotions or feelings of infatuation, I stuck to my crush. I believed in Kanye beyond feelings. I had little hope to believe in him year after year, but I believed in it. Many times I began to hate him and even dought him, but he continued to give me reasons to hold on. This was enough for me to raise up my hands and say fuck it. If I didn't say fuck it before, I said fuck it now. We were talking and laughing and making plans and this is your plan of loving me. On top of that he started making songs for Kim. I was so fucking done with Kanye. You know what I would have liked? The truth. I didn't want to hear bits and pieces anymore. I wanted to hear the truth. I would always give Kanye time and space to speak up about certain things, but not anymore. I began asking him questions and he would give me these half ass answers and that would piss me off even more. He would tell me to calm down and that my anger was affecting him. Did it look like I cared. I didn't want to hear anything that he had to say anymore.

He started to not respond to me. Maybe it was because I only speak negative to him about Kim. Maybe he stopped talking to me because I was cursing his ass out every day. He never said. Either way, we weren't talking anymore and I would go home and cry the night away. Many nights, many weeks I would go home and cry. I was sad that he wasn't talking to me anymore. I would cry because all I ever wanted I started to believe was over. It was everywhere in the media that Kanye was with the so called love of his life. How could I have been so blind? Well when people lie, I guess that's possible.

I would put my heart into my films. I would express my feelings on camera. Even thou it would appear as funny, it was really how I was feeling. The media spoke on my feelings and I would hope that I could take him away from Kim. I felt I was more of a lady and a good girl. I believed that I deserved him, not her. The naked video posted with me in was about Kanye, but Kim's porn was with another man. I'm thinking, "Why would Kanye pick a porn star after admitting he made the wrong choice picking a stripper". I was so done with this crush on Kanye. I guess I didn't want to let go because of the years I invested. I didn't want to let go because of the dreams that I believed in. But this was truly it. I was still somehow riding off my name. I was still using the name Mrs. Kanye West but I'd let people know how I felt through my art. I didn't quite give it all up. I just went from happy bride to angry bride. I still wanted to work with Kanye, but was 100% done being celibate or believing that our love was anything real. I didn't believe in Kanye's heart anymore. I wasn't sure before if I would be with Kanye West or not because of the lack of information. He rarely came outright blunt to say "yes" or "no". I just didn't want to let go all of those years. But I was sure after that, that I was done.

I was sure after talking to him all of those months that he'd love me for real and yet he pulled a stunt like that. I felt he didn't care, so neither did I. It was one thing when I had more reasons to believe. But now I felt I had all the reasons not to believe. I held on to Kanye for love. I didn't hold on to Kanye to hope for the rest of my life. It started to seem like all

I was fucking doing was holding on to him. I was finally ready to let go and enjoy love. I didn't want to wait for it anymore. I started to feel like I could get better treatment from other men. I stopped believing that Kanye was the only man that could give me affection and royal treatment. I was so fucking ready to move on.

Let her know she can have it Keyshia Cole, Enough of No Love

CHAPTER ELEVEN

"Falling in Love With Someone Else"

It was until 2013 that I realized how I was chasing men. Maybe in the back of my mind I knew that I was doing it, but I guess I wasn't paying much attention. Growing up and moving from foster home to foster home I always felt like I had to prove that I was good enough to live with people. In order to keep the family that I was placed with I had to be a certain way or my caseworker would give me a 14 day notice and I'd have to go to another foster home. I look back and realize that I grew up trying to prove to people that I was good enough over and over. I cry as I think about it. It is the reason why I have a habit of going out of my way to prove men my worth. It's funny because the men that I like are the ones that prefer chasing woman. Don't get me wrong, I love that. I just was unaware of my behavior. I didn't realize that I was chasing. I knew that I had a big heart and that no one could forget me once they met me, but I didn't see it as a bad thing. I wasn't too happy realizing that. I want to be with an aggressive man. I want us to be in the car and he put his hands on my leg. He kisses me because he adores me. But I can only get that by being passive. I would be passive in the beginning of the friendships, but if it seemed too good to be true I would prove my love out of fear.

I always knew what I wanted out of a man and I always knew how to treat one. However, I was unaware of how clingy and aggressive I was toward them. It was until this year that I fell in love with someone new that I saw all of my bad habits. Of course I'm aware of my aggression towards Kanye but because I'm an artist, I felt that it was okay to do what I was doing because of how I was doing it. I was doing things artistically like making songs, wearing costumes and making films. Most people express their feelings through art as well, so I only saw it as being creative. Apart of why I went out of my way to express how I felt for Kanye had to do with the fact that I couldn't just ask him by walking to his house and ringing his bell. I felt I had to do whatever it took to be seen by him and not overlooked. But now I see the light! So, let's cut the crap. I was chasing him too. But I feel free. Now that I see that I was doing these things and now that I see that it was wrong, I'm up for change.

Your child hood development shapes you into who you are. As a child, life molds you as you grow. It becomes easy to do what you do consistently and it becomes a habit. So it became normal for me to prove to someone that I was good enough instead of just being good enough. I guess that's why I can be a street performer. Most people wouldn't bother but being a street performer takes courage. Half the time people don't give a fuck. You can sound like Whitney and Mariah but people are not receptive to your talent as they are if they bought tickets to see you in concert. It always takes some self-confidence out of this fucking world to sing to people who give you this unbelievable vibe. When I'm singing if they aren't feeling me I think to myself, "I'M TALENTED AS FUCK, FUCK A HATER"! I get my money so I feel it's worth it. I must admit it takes some real courage to be heard on the streets. Most people may choose not to street perform because they don't have the time to prove shit. I got to the point where I started looking at the wall after being mentally tired of

2004

Jackson
DAN FLAVIN
Energy to help you stay in the Loop.
CHAI
TOWN

2005

2006

2007

2008

2009

2010

News

2011

2012

KANYE
WEST

Jackson
300S
0E/0W

Jackson
iPad

2013

Jackson

performing day in and day out on the streets. Just recently I performing like I use to. I focus on what's going on in my life and sing with passion. To some degree we all have to prove our self-worth, but I'm not proving to shit to anyone, anymore. I'm not proving it to a man and I'm especially not proving it while singing on the streets.

Okay yea, I will let the man lead and will follow his ass to Paris. Whenever there is a sign of discord in the friendship I'd normally go out my way to prove that my love was real to the highest degree. In the past that's when things would go left.

I started learning this when I got sprung with someone new. At the end of 2012, I was still in love with Kanye and was working on my movie about him. I reconnected with Matthew who played on my first film as Kanye in 2010. But unlike before, we slept together. I was no longer being celibate and I was done hoping and wishing that Kanye would be there for me. I starting having ambition, feeling like

I could get things done without Kanye. I surely wasn't going to wait on him to be the only one to kiss me anymore. I wanted to be kissed right then and there. It's a lot of men out here with the right touch. Unlike before I started to realize that someone closer could give me the things that I waited for Kanye West to give. I loved Kanye still but I wished him God speed. He had him a family and was flaunting it on T.V so no point in me playing stupid.

I started to change my TV screen name from Mrs. Kanye West to my now legal name, Kanyeresa West. I was still holding Kanye down but in a different way. I waited years for a family as a child and finally got it. I waited 7 years for Kanye to love me, to kiss me and be there for me and was done waiting for the same thing to happen. I was kind of mad that I invested my youth to a fantasy instead of living it up. My twenties are dam near gone. I spent it not having sex and not being held. I was around men but mostly only when I was performing. The biggest thing I tried to avoid was regret. While I was waiting for Kanye I didn't want to let go. As the days went by I would hold on to the days before.What I want more now than anything is a family. For me to want a family from Kanye is kind of delusional to most people's point of view, I bet. There was more to this crush than just me thou. But even thou Kanye provoked some of my feelings, it's still kind of stupid for me to have held on for so long. I should have played smarter. In the end, all I want is a family and to belong. I was about to learn that I was doing all the wrong things to get it done. I could have had a husband and kids years before. To be honest, I didn't want that back then. I only wanted it from Kanye because I had fell in love with him. After my first marriage at 18 years old, the last thing I wanted was family. All I wanted was to be a singer. All I wanted to do was sing. I'm so good at it and never had the tolerance for anything in life but for art. I did not graduate from grammar school and I definitely did not graduate from high school. I would sit in the bathroom stall listening to headphones instead of going to class. Growing up not feeling loved majority of the time, music was my best friend.

At first I didn't want to be circled around people. All

I wanted to do was sing, be alone and make my own money. I had that so I guess I'm tired of that. Even thou I imagined the life of getting out of shofars, limos, and living in a condo, I still lived a very comfortable life street performing. I was doing what I loved but it was different. People don't support street performers like they do people with talent on the big screen, which is sad. A street performer can have an amazing talent, but the first thing people do when they see a street performer is look around to see what the fuck others are thinking. Stupid brainless people! Now if it's a crowd already formed when they arrive, they're they are clapping with they fake and phony ass! It's funny how people don't think for themselves. When I'm singing and people check for others before they choose to respond, I laugh inside. I'm bold enough to stand in such a strange place to do what I love without caring about what others think and here they are pretending to be dignified but yet need others approval to choose what they like. I know I can sing. I can sing my ass off! I have an amazing voice! The passion inside of my performances are evident. I can't dance worth a lick but it's not my dream to dance. They can stereo type that people have to know how to dance if they are really talented but they can also stereotype if I got nuts under my pants. My performances on the big stage would be something different. Kanye may never admit it, but he was inspired by me using ballerinas. It's a compliment if you ask me. Kanye and I may have only seen each other once but we shared so many different things in a phenomenal way.

Hood phenomenon; the LeBron of rhyme, Devil In a new dress

It's 2013 now and I feel I've done all the trying to make a better living that I could do. Doctors can go to school and so can teachers, but as a musician even if you go to school you still need that almighty dollar behind you. In the music industry, they don't hire you like they hire doctors in the hospitals. There's a saying that goes, it's not what you know, it's who you know. That statement is so true. Well I'm done trying so hard to make it all happen. I want family now. Feeling alone, I'm tired of protecting myself and tired of doing it all by myself. I want someone to protect me and be there for me. Want to enjoy a man's love and pick a new career. I may be good at what I do, but I don't want to wake up at 50 years old realizing how far my ambitions really are taking me. It's clear when Kanye chose to date Kim after making multiple promises to me, that he just may never keep those promises. I wanted regular life. I wanted to feel like love was right here and not far away. I went from chasing a career to chasing a man and it didn't feel good anymore.

I wanted excitement back in my life. The only excitement I experienced the last 7 years was the thought of it happening. But what was really happening? I would spend my money to do this and I would spend my money to do that, but what was I gaining? Was I gaining the things that I so desired and was working hard for? Where was my pink and purple house that I wanted? Where was my name at on the billboard charts? You know what thou; "they are lucky I wasn't on the billboard charts because I would have always been number one!" I'm too talented musically to be less than that. In the music that I produced I must admit could have been so much better, but I could do what my money would allow me to do. If I had money invested in me to make a complete album, it would have been the best r&b and pop album of all fucking time!

But here I am at 29 without a contract and without a record deal. I wanted to make it in the industry as young as possible after watching Brandy, Usher and Monica, and hearing about Michael Jackson's legacy. Doing it young was your only chance, I thought. I believe differently now thou. The first two winners on "The Voice" were in their 30's. 2 chainz is in his 40's. My idols Kanye, Beyonce and Jay are in their 30's and 40's. I guess age isn't a big thing as I once thought. However, I'm through reaching. I want that agape love. I want the love that loves you no matter what. The love when a man is more into you than you are into him. A love that's right here, that I don't have to wait for.

A 24 karate is a beautiful thing, but what's more precious is my love for this thing –Miss Flow/Kanyeresa, Gonna Make It

Things are different now. I would choose love at this point over a record deal. I want both, but if I had to choose it would be a relationship. Now let me finish telling you about the look alike Matthew who played the role in my film as KanYe West. I was very attracted to Matthew. He reminded me so much of Kanye. There was this electrifying energy between us. I wanted him to fuck me so bad and he did. So, we made plans to do just that. He fucked me so many times and so good all in one night. We did a lot of kissing and caressing. He held me afterwards which felt so good and so right. It felt so good to be fucked again. I wanted him every night and all the time.

I didn't hear from him for a week and was feening and craving him inside of me. I called him and called him and called him. Eventually he got back to me and told me that something had happened with his phone. He was willing to come over that night thou, so it was all good. We fucked and we fucked but not as before. I was led to believe he had so much energy the first time because maybe it was a while since he last had sex. Either way the sex was good. He held me again. I caressed his head and his face while watching a movie. I was asking him was he okay a lot. I was trying to make sure that he was comfortable. I guess I asked him too many times because I heard agitation in his voice. After that I remained quiet. I didn't feel free with him anymore because he seemed distant all of a sudden. I was wondering what was wrong, but I was soon to find out. Sex felt so good with him. We kissed passionately and out of all the one night stands I had in the past, I wouldn't embrace the guys or kiss them. Even with Eric we didn't really kiss. I was under the impression that we had a sensual connection and were feeling each other.

I thought men loved affection. I thought men love attention. I thought men loved to be caressed and assured. They say what you don't know won't hurt you. That quote must be for only cheating because I wish I knew how much I DID NOT KNOW about men. Brian sent a text telling me that "I was being too mushy and he was just trying to enjoy casual sex". "Casual sex"? I asked him. "Do people kiss during casual sex", I asked him sarcastically. "It's how he fuck", he replied. "Oh no he didn't ", I thought". Well, I'm so much different than before. Before I would blow up a man's phone calling him consistently. I have more pride now. Fuck him!

One day I tried to contact him about the movie that I needed him for, but there was no response within a week. When I sent him a "fuck him" text, he replied to that. "Aint that bout a bitch"! I dogged his ass clean out! "How I ended up on his work table with him inside of me, fucking me, I don't know. I think I just landed there, maybe. It was beginning to be like a whip appeal thing. It would be intense and oh god it felt so good. He was sitting in his chair picking movies for us to watch looking regular, but you know when your sexually into someone, they look dam good to you. His sex took me to a place I had not been in a long time. After the sex was over, he didn't call. Once again he was distant and I didn't like the way needing him felt. I wanted him to want the sex as much as I did. I was talking to everyone about Matthew, trying to figure out what the fuck to do. My first thought was to sleep with other men so it wouldn't bother me.

On Jackson Street, January 5th I was talking to my close friend Crystal. She's a free spirited woman who don't take any junk. She's a janitor for CTA. CTA is the company that owns the rail and buses in Chicago. I was telling her that I probably just need to sleep with someone to take my mind off of him. And omfg this sexy ass man walked past us while we were talking. I kid you not he looked so fucking good! He had a dog with him and he was in uniform. I saw the uniform before, but not his sexy ass in it. Right away I knew he was a k9 officer. K9 is a company hired by CTA to protect passengers that ride the trains.

As soon as I saw him I started flirting. The more I flirted, the more he smiled and the more he smiled, the more I flirted. He had the sexiest smile I had ever seen. I mean he was very, very handsome. I just remember looking at him thinking, "Yummy".

I forgot all about Crystal that day. We usually have great conversations while she cleans Jackson Street spotless, but I was interested in talking to dark chocolate.

His name was Dwight. I never met a Dwight before. It was such a unique name. He had sexy ass lips and a perfect face, a nice height and a sexy ass swag. We started talking immediately, having great conversations. We talked a lil about his present life and I asked him for his advice concerning Matthew. I told him that he didn't like me rubbing his head and shit like that. I demonstrated to him how I would rub it and he loved it. He told me that he would never make me stop touching him like that if I did that to him. I noticed he was saying all the right things that I liked to hear. He was easy to talk to and easy to laugh with. He didn't judge me and he was just so cool to be around.

I let him know that I performed there on the subway. It was amazing that we never crossed paths. He worked for K-9 three years prior and it was my 9 year singing on Jackson, yet we never seen each other before.

I began to sing. That was the first day that I ever felt so protected while being down there. When I began to sing, he loved it. I sang Beyoncé's "Dance for you". I don't think I noticed a K9 officer until that day. I use to love it when they were on Jackson years before, but I didn't pay them much mind after awhile. I did notice one guy who would always have my back. He was quick to remove someone for me, but I clearly saw Dwight. I liked him but I didn't think much about it. I didn't think it would go far at all especially after he told me that he had a girl. I planned to just be cool with him. I don't like being second. I mean, no one does. I warned him about the things that the media said about me. I wanted him to be aware of my Kanye West crush. I was over being true to Kanye, but something in me still loved him. He was still first in my heart.

Days later Dwight called to tell me that he left his girl. When we talked on the phone prior, something was just right about him. I couldn't see yet just what it was, but he just seemed so perfect to me. Days later, we began to chill outside of Jackson. I told him I was looking for someone to film me for a show that I was doing, "The Love Video Countdown". The "Love Video Countdown" is a show that I host love videos for in New York and Chicago. He didn't mind filming me even after I warned him that I would only be in a t-shirt and panties. Shit, who wouldn't wanna see that. Now that he wasn't with his girl, I wouldn't mind taking it there. After Matthew thou, I said that I was going to follow Steve Harvey's 90 day rule.

The day he came to my apartment, he had this ora about him that wasn't intimidating. It was just so relaxing to be around Dwight. Unlike Matthew, he

Jurassic

was easy to laugh with and easy to talk to. Watching him while he taped me was so enticing. I counted 87, 88, 89, and fuck it, that day was the 90th. I was like fuck the 90 day rule! I didn't plan on taking him or any guy serious anyways.

I was announcing videos and shaking my ass on camera. In the middle of the taping, he took his finger and touched my vagina and I just couldn't resist. No one caressed me in such a long time. I didn't have anything but the 90 day rule holding me back. I loved kissing him. I loved the way his lips felt. He had the softest touch. I liked him. Fuck, I began to like him a lot. He seemed like he'd be a lot of fun. But I had no idea I was about to fall in love.

Dwight Austin Demery Jr. is his name. D.j for short. He can't stand when I announce his entire name, but oh well its not like it's not on google. He stand at about 5'11, caramel dark with the sexiest lips I've ever kissed. So I let him fuck me, kiss me and hold me til I fell asleep.

Right before I met him and Matthew, I had just got back into town. I rented out a room in an apartment building. Every time I rented, someone was somehow a covering for me, keeping me in check, making sure I payed the rent on time. My ex, Kevin was almost always at my place in 2005. With Kevin as my angel, it was easy for me to keep my head strong when it came to paying the rent. I payed rent to my cousin, grandmother, god mother and some friends years prior. I knew what I was doing, but was use to some kind of guidance. Living on my own for the first time in a long time, I did what I had to do to make rent. I would sing and save my money.

Thanksgiving was when I came back from New York in 2012. I was in New York the entire summer. Now that I was home, I would wake up early in the morning and hustle singing on Jackson Street, Subway. Even thou I was paying rent, I would need money to eat. I didn't have many people to ask. The people that I could ask, I did not want to. I somehow gained the courage to ask Dwight if he could help me. This happened on 3 occasions. He would give me money, take me out to eat and wouldn't dare take me to just any place. He would ask me what I wanted. I would tell him I preferred him to take me somewhere that he wouldn't spend a lot of money. He insisted to take me to the place that I desired. I thought that was so sweet, but even thou he didn't mind I really didn't want him to go out his way for me. I can't lie thou, I thought much of him when he was doing that. I mean, I liked him for more than his money gestures. He was just my type all around.

One morning I asked him to feed me and he took me to a restaurant for breakfast. Man, I was loving him. Normally when I went to that restaurant I would be alone, but not that day. I remember how easy it was to sit across from him. I loved looking at him. I loved hearing whatever it was he had to say. The biggest thing I began to love about Dwight was listening to the things that he did and did not agree with. I was so wrapped up into the media and how Hollywood do things, but listening to him was listening to a person with morals. Hearing him talk was relaxing. It wasn't all about Gucci and gold. I mean don't get me wrong, that has its place. It wasn't like he came across like an old man who was just strict about life. He has a wild side too, but as I listened to him he put those things in perspective. He just had more values than what I was use to, which was great in my eyes. His dominance and aggression made me feel like a lady with just his presence alone.

After we ate at the restaurant that morning we agreed to watch movies, but you know what we ended up doing. Even thou it was so soon, I wanted him. I wanted a lot of him. Since I was so picky about the guys I did not want, I felt if I did want them I could probably have them.

All I knew was that this dude was cool and I wanted him to stay in my life. He was bringing back fun in my world. I was smiling for real from within. He made me happier than I was on any trip to New York, Florida, California, or anywhere. I was really feeling him the more I was around him. We would passionately kiss and talk about everything. We could laugh and joke with each other about anything. Everything would flow so free and easy between us. Being with him like the feeling I was seeking from Kanye West without the record deal.

My favorite thing about being with Dwight was that our feelings were mutual. He explained that we were just friends, but it didn't matter to me. A title didn't have anything to do with the way that he made me feel. If he would have been talking about being my boyfriend so soon it would have ran me away anyways. So, I was felling his decision.

I enjoyed D.J picking me up after I would sing. After all this time that I was performing on the subway, he was the first guy to pick me up and take me home. I never would ask anyone to take me home and they would never offer. Doing things so new and so fun with Dwight was making me feel so special. It's was a lot of guys who wanted to do that for me and more, but it takes a special guy to rub me the right way. I honestly loved going over his house more than

I did going to my apartment. I loved riding with him in his car, playing cards with him and his cousin. I loved watching movies with him. The fun thing we were doing was pictures of our moments. At first I wouldn't dare take a picture of me and a guy. I would protect my image. If I took pictures, I would be in the picture by myself. It was fun how he didn't object to so much. He was so free around me like I was free around him. I was doing so many exciting things that 16 years old do at the age 29 with D.J.

Maybe I was comfortable being alone because D.C.F.S sheltered me growing up. It obviously took the right person to take me out of my shell and D.J was doing that.

I'd sing on the subway and through bad moments, contemplate on him and begin to smile. He was too good to be true. It was too good to be true. But I refused to dought that this could be the beginning of something great and something better than what I ever had. He'd tell me he wasn't going anywhere which made me feel secure. He was doing things like offering to teach me how to drive. He'd promise to take me to nice places and we even planned excitement for both our birthdays.

I fell hard for D.J because he opened my eyes to a part of life that I refused to see, the simple life. I could have been dating, fucking, and having my fun, but I chose to be alone and chase my dreams. I was starting to regret that. I started to do the opposite of being obsessed with Kanye West. I went to the courts to start the process of changing my name back. I almost didn't write this book because I didn't want my Kanye West image to emasculate him. That's a word he used to describe my crush dealing with Kanye. He said that if a girl is into someone who is a famous rapper and has a regular guy, it can emasculate him because he don't have as much money as him. I wanted D.J to know that even if Kanye and Kim were were over and I finally did have the chance, for no money or record deal would I compromise what we shared.

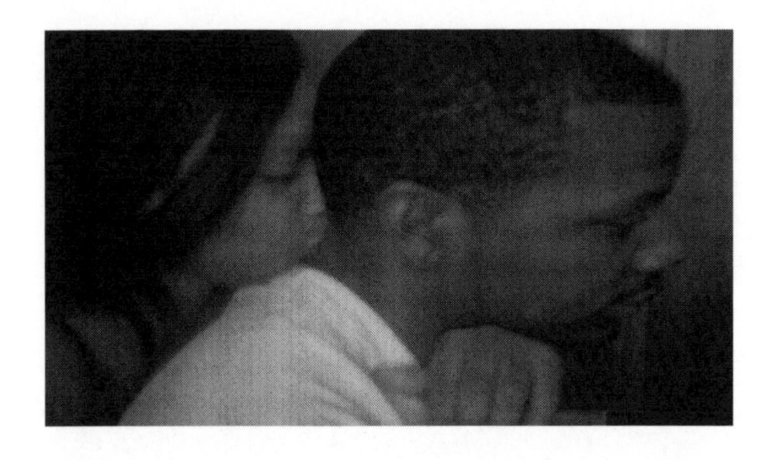

He and I shared something so special that people with millions of dollars don't experience, pure chemistry. There are guys that I liked before, but it wasn't easy to kiss them. It wasn't easy to rub their face. Our chemistry was like living in the 1700's. We didn't need a Wii game. We didn't need a Nintendo Game. Being around each other was enough. Don't get me wrong, we had fun watching movies and doing all those things technology offers, but we didn't NEED it. **I'm not sure if he felt like this with someone else, I just know that I didn't.** I loved everything that was happening. While I was singing on Jackson he would embrace and protect me the entire time and after work he'd be there to pick me up. We had fun agreeing and disagreeing. Whether we were in his covers or mine we would have the greatest sex ever. So why the fuck would he want to compromise that? Why would he run from that? I never expected him to end it or walk away from me. This love was too rich to end in my eyes.

I did not want to let Dwight go. Being around him was changing me. He never told me not to be naked in front of the camera or to stop cursing people out. It was just things that he would say or suggest that started convicting me to do so. Chasing the music business and chasing Kanye was my way of being aggressive as I found myself being as a child. But Dwight loving me made me feel like the girl I always wanted to feel like. It's the way my dad would make me feel. Something that I'd never forget D.J telling me that he'd stab a nigga with his keys for me.

We grew a little a part because he started sleeping with other woman and th at's when I started acting different. I was trying not to trip, but it would say "mad" in some of the things that I was doing. We slowly lost our spark and I hated it. I mean I was so angry! I cried because I just didn't like the way I was feeling again. No way did I think a regular nigga could take me off my square again. I was caught into Hollywood that I forgot how regular dudes can get you going crazy for them too. I just knew I had it under control. "I'm older so I got this", I was thinking. I was thinking that now I had enough strength to not cry over spoiled milk. I can let go and move on to the next one. But emotions and memories of the most beautifulist moments can be hard to let go sometimes. I would tell yourself over and over how possible it it was to make things the way that they were.

I learned so much about myself during this time than I ever did before. At least it seemed that way. I always knew what I wanted my perfect man to look and talk like. What I should have been doing iwas analyze myself. I was specific about the guys I wanted. However, I believed that because I was beautiful, affectionate and have the greatest tendency to be faithful, I felt that was all I needed to be for a man. Ha, who was I kidding?

So many women like me are just too aggressive for the man we most likely seek. Women like me crave affection, protection and love. We desire men who are emotionally strong. I want the kind of guy who can hold him own. The kind of guy that is nothing like a woman. So why would a man want a woman who behaves like a man? Even the most beautifulist woman can be so manly, so dominate, and so aggressive. That turns an aggressive man off. It's obvious that woman behave like that being use to protecting themselves, being the one that had to be their own father through childhood. Maybe as an adult we had to be the man in our lives. Maybe we had no other choice but to find ourselves aggressively independent. Some men are turned on by a woman's independence but are shocked when they see the same woman have such a wall up during tough times. Don't get it twisted; if she's aggressive she has issues of putting up walls like a man.

When you first meet me and I like you, I do have all my walls down. I have yet to meet someone who did not purposely or selfishly keep me from putting them walls right back up. The real me can be shown when someone does their best at loving me. Until someone loves me for real, everyone will see the pain of my past. But what I do know now? Unlike before when I was being loyal to Kanye, I want and NEED to be around men. I know that being around men gives me a reason to keep my hair done. Men keep me feeling like a girl. It's not that I need to sleep with different men or be a hoe to be around them. You know what thou, I don't even believe in the word hoe. Life is what it is. You horny, want to sleep around, that's yo business. Be safe, protect yourself and be discreet. I didn't believe that before Kim starting Kanye. But after holding out for so long and it failing, shit I don't believe in all that bullshit of waiting anymore.

I want a good man by my side, the kind of man that I like. The kind that is aggressive and stern. The kind that is loving and easy for me to share my heart to. And if I want him to want to be with me, I realized just this year that chasing a man is not the way to get it done. When I was chasing Kanye, I felt it was okay because it was mixed with art and it was also dealing with my career. I thought it was cute. Now I know that, that is just the way I was use to doing things.

Every man that I liked I feared him walking out my life. I would also believe that they wanted to be secure and I would go to the extreme to secure them.

At 29 I am just learning how that is not cute. Yea I believe in sitting in a chair, crossing my legs and hope that the guy would walk over and ask for my number, instead of me approaching him. But I just noticed how after my relationships would start, I would chase the man to keep the man. That came to an end this year.

When me and D.J had our moments where we did not speak, I would not call him and call him and call him. And when I saw him, I would still give him his space. In the beginning of our friendship I was doing a bit much and that's when I looked in the mirror and saw what I was doing and I stopped. I never meant harm but I also did not know how much a turn off it was when I would go out my way to prove love. As a lady, I see it's best to fall back and let him take the wheel, even through fear. I don't have to prove to him my beauty, he should just see it.

Around the same time that I heard Kanye's baby news, I met D.J. It didn't even bother me because I was having so much fun with Dwight. I refused to let D.J go even after we became distant. I was scared I'd go back to that dumb fantasy lie I was living. I knew I probably would to have something to hold on to. I also didn't want to end up with someone who wasn't as good as Dwight. Some men who have good sex don't have good sense and some men who have perfect bank accounts don't have good sense.

I loved our friendship. When one needed, the other was there. When one needed to talk, the other was there to listen. But here I am in New York and I am still much into Dwight and I haven't let him go. I came to New York because I came to sue Kanye for the contract that he promised me. There is no love lost between me and Kanye, I just want my contract! I love Kanye differently now thou. That's Kim man and I respect that. I will always have nothing but good things to say about him. I have the utmost respect for Kanye because he is the inspiration behind me as Miss Flow and as Kanyeresa West.

Kanye West's music, videos, and concerts play a big part in who I am as a performer. The way that I see my dreams are impacted by things that I seen Yeezy do. I'm more focused on his art, not the critics. Fuck critics, well always have 'em. They can be fun at times, but yet we all have them. We are all critics, and for that reason I never want to prove myself to people again, not in art and not for love. Take me as I am like Mary J say's or have nothing at all.

I'm waiting for Yeezy's next album. I'm so excited. I can't lie. Don't get me wrong I love the Good Music album, but after hearing the collaboration with Jay, I was anticipating a solo album. Word in town is that he's working on it. YES! I'm so excited to hear it and I am so ready to buy the best rapper in the world's next album!

When it comes to being a friend to D.J, I believe I can do chase my dreams and be his friend. Instead of giving up my dreams I can have success in the music and film industry and have D.J too. Things will get better, I just know it. I don't mean to intimidate a man by the way that I look up to Kanye, but they have no idea the history.

Within this little time of knowing D.j I see the wall that he has, but I see the love that he has as well. I believe that it will get better. No pressure from me. I just adore how he brings out the lady in me. I see the importance of things that I have overlooked for so long by listening to his point of views.

It may seem a little odd for me to say this but I don't want to live my life without D.J's friendship. I knew what kind of person Rick Party would be in my life by listening to him on the radio. Ten years later, he's been the greatest dad and I do not regret meeting him. He did so many things for me as a child that took away a lot of fears and pain. I guess after living in 25 different foster homes and group homes you have a good instinct about people. Dealing with so many different personalities, I can read people really well.

If I had to choose between my career and D.J, it would be D.J. I came to New York to get some air and finish writing this book. And now that I'm at the end of writing it, I'm headed back to Chicago to see his handsome face.

What' the sense of trying hard to find your dreams without someone to share em with, tell me what does it mean? Run To You, Whitney Houston

As far as my tattoos and my name change is concerned, I will keep them because I will always love the greatest rapper ever, Kanye West.

CHAPTER TWELVE

"YEEZY TAUGHT ME"

Before there was a Lady Gaga there was Kanye West. Before rappers did things out of the ordinary, it was Kanye West who set the trends. At first it was just about being a hip-hop artist and being lyrical. It was KanYe West who made people feel that it's okay to say fuck the world's opinion and do what you believe. Kanye West, the rapper who rock teddy bears and who wear masks is someone who made history already. It was KanYe West the rapper who was the first major artist that made an entire album singing. In August, 2008 KanYe West released an album entitled "808's and Heartbreaks". He sang on the entire album. The music had a different sound than what was playing on the radio at the time. KanYe West told people through live performances and interviews that the album was inspired from things he was going through. He wasn't concerned about sales or what people thought. He felt like making the album and that's what he did. It was Kanye West who made me feel that it was okay to do the weird shit that was floating in the back of my head. Every artistic thing starts somewhere. People teach others that if it's weird, "omg don't do that"! But fuck that! I'm sure it wasn't easy for people to grasp the idea of the first guitar, piano, and flute when it was first created. Everything starts from somewhere.

Jay-Z inspired me not to be ashamed anymore about street performing. When I thought street performing was stupid, Jay-Z lyrics inspired me that it was okay. Jay-Z turning his hustle into millions of dollars and success made me feel that it was okay to start from there.

Me, turn that $62 to $125, $125 to $250, $250 to a half a man aint nothing nobody can do with me Clique, Jay-Z

But Kanye West is the heart of my entire career. Even thou I date other people now and gave up my dreams of being his girl, I will always wear his name in honor. It is he who inspired me. I know it seems on my TV show that I'm upset at him, but deep down I will always love Kanye West. All the times that I stayed closed to everything that he was doing, I learned that doing the unthinkable was okay. I learned that there is nothing wrong with creating new art. People in society normally follow things that are already hot. But someone started that hotness and Kanye West is one of them. People can make you feel that if it's not hot then it's not going to be. I see people when they see me singing on the subway, mindless. They look around to see if anyone else is enjoying my beautiful talent before they decide to enjoy it. I sound better than many artists sound. "What the fuck you need approval from people for"? I sound good enough for you to watch and tip me! That's this generation for you thou. In history books it seems people stood with pride with what they believed from years before. Now it seems that majority of people are with the n-crowd. But Kanye West tell people on stage during his concerts to "think for your fucking self". Kanye West taught me that being creative is okay.

There are a lot of things that Kanye West encouraged me not to do. It Is because of him that I don't smoke weed anymore. I have a rich sound when I sing by staying away from drugs and alcohol. That is one of the few things that Kanye West taught me. He's one of the first rappers to cross-over into the pop culture. He is the same person people didn't even wanna believe in.

A&R's looking like pshh we messed up now Diamonds, KanYe West

I feel free to do new things because of KanYe West. The things that others convince themselves not to do, Kanye's music and art have taught me that it's okay to.

WHO TAUGHT YOU HOW TO DO THAT GIRL?

-YEEZY TAUGHT ME

From the author,

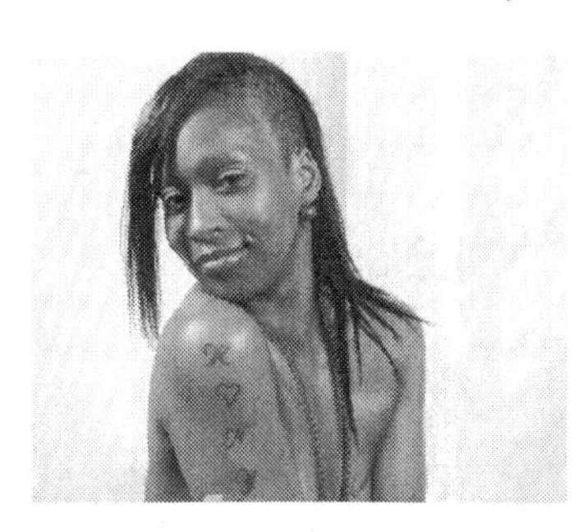

The way I see life is amazing. I view it much different than I did years ago. I learned a lot about being happy and even more about having faith. Yes, I was truly head over heels in love with Kanye West. As amazing as my story sounds, I'm more positive now then I was when I was all about him. I'm not as angry because I love myself more now. People say "love yourself" all that time, but now I see what it really means. It's also good to have a man around because he chose you. It's even better when there's happiness between you two. I learned to not only believe in something, but to embrace it. I believe in love. I believe in true love. I believe in internal love. Internal love is a chemistry that you have with someone whether you're in Paris or at a subway train station. External love is not everything. It's cool to be seen and it's nice to be noticed, but it's better to be happy on the inside. When you grow with someone who truly makes you happy it's better than just appraisal for your image. After the appraisal for your image, do those people care for you? Will those people ride or die for you? Ya see, I did all that I did for Kanye because I wanted to. I fell in love with Kanye West because it fucking happened. And now that I'm in love with another man I have that same energy towards him minus the tattoos.

But whenever I sing **“I Will Always Love You”,** I’m singing about KanYe West.

I’ll think of you every step of the way. I hope you have all you dreamed of. I wish to you joy and happiness, but above all this I wish to you love. I’ll Always Love You, Dolly Pardon

Thanks for reading, much love

-KanYeresa West

Linda met KanYe West backstage and sang to him in front of thousands of people. She was silent about her crush for years but when she finally opened up her feelings for him, she tattoed his name 5 times on her body and changed her name to his.

-Obsessed with KanYe West

8918516R00135

Printed in Great Britain
by Amazon.co.uk, Ltd.,
Marston Gate.